Getting ThERE

Getting ThERE

*Thespians, Two Cats,
and Deliverance*

Alternative takes on
"This American Life."

Thomas Allen Childers

Paperback ISBN 978-0-9986449-6-7
Library of Congress Control Number:2020939347

To John, and to the memory of my parents, Jeannette and Allen.

Acknowledgments

Although they are blameless for it, three people were essential to this volume: my husband, John Hall, for his da capo support and willingness to appear on many of its pages, unexpurgated. Caitlin Fitzgerald, who voiced encouragement, nosed out the right word, and eagle-eyed my Oxford commas. And Janet Falon, whose years of teaching, coaching, cheerleading, and prodding brought it about. Thank you, thank you, thank you.

TABLE OF CONTENTS

Up Front

In a white clapboard farmhouse in southern Ohio, outside Rio Grande (rye-o grand) I met Grandmother's kitchen. That's where I started down the food path.

"Grandmother" was my father's mother, Daisy Childers. I was probably five or six when I noticed her kitchen for the first time. There was no electricity, or gas. Nor was there plumbing—not ever, as long as my grandparents lived there. The major appliances were a four-burner wood stove, an icebox on the front porch, a hand pump under the grape arbor, and Grandmother.

The kitchen was always warm. Warmth emanated from the stove, from the activity of Grandmother's cooking, and from Grandmother herself. Some of it came from her active body and some of it must surely have been love, although I didn't recognize that at the time. There was visual warmth, too, in the reds and yellows of the floral print on the feed-sack cotton she wore. She would pick out a pattern, and Granddaddy would buy enough sacks of feed in that pattern for her to make a dress. She turned the remnants into aprons and bonnets.

I loved her food. For Sunday dinner, after catching a chicken, beheading it, scalding it, plucking it, and butchering it, she fried it in butter and made a white gravy with lots of pepper. There were always mashed potatoes, scraped into the serving dish by the "spatula" of her first two fingers to form a white volcano oozing black-peppered butter.

She would serve beet-juice-pickled eggs and pork-greasy green beans, and slices of anemic-colored but intensely flavored tomato as big as a saucer. For breakfast, she might produce re-fried "rib meat"—pieces of pork rib that she'd put up in the fall—and a couple of fried eggs fresh from the hen. I always turned down her offer of cereal because I didn't like milk. But one morning she persuaded me to try oatmeal with a dab of cream that Granddaddy had just brought in from the cow, by way of the milk separator. I converted instantly.

Everything she turned out—with the niggling exception of her bland sugar cookies—was A to A+. The ingredients were fresh and unadulterated and the cooking, straightforward and delicious.

The "fresh and unadulterated" side of the larder was augmented at the general store in town, or at the Jewel Tea "rolling store." Jewel Tea was like a bookmobile of food—a motorized grocery van that came to the house once a week so Grandmother could trade eggs for staples like flour and sugar and for certain non-fresh and adulterated foods like canned soups and baked beans. We ate these store-bought things, but I never counted them as Grandmother's cooking.

She generated exotica, too. One day—I was probably 12 or so—she asked if she could fry me a chicken head. I said yes, and she did. It was my first chicken head. Floured and fried in pork fat, it tasted like crisp-fried chicken skin, which is about all it is. What's not to like? And she often served a dessert that I assumed was beet pie, because the filling was deep red. I learned later that it was peach pie, made from the red-fleshed fruit of two blood-peach ("Blue George") trees that shared space in the side yard with the rusting hulk of a Model A Ford.

Fried chicken heads and red peach pie could grab the attention of a little kid. It was probably at that point—excited by the aromas and tastes and mouth-feel of new foods from Grandmother's kitchen, and anticipating food discoveries yet to come—that my adventure with eating began.

When I began noodling around with memoirish writing, I didn't know where it was heading. I started out wanting to record memory before I lost it and, beyond that, to eke out memory that was in hiding, such as the images and stories of my mother, which had faded since her death.

After a couple of years of writing this and that, the pieces began to mass. If I envisioned them stacked up, they took on the semblance of a—good lord!—a book. And a book needs a moniker.

Early on, I meant all the writings to be related to food—not surprising, given the powerful inspiration of Grandmother's cooking. If I had left it at that, a title would have come readily, like *Home on the Range, Fooders' Guide to Life, The Willing Palate, A Foodie's Progress*. Readily, if not brilliantly.

But as I struggled to remember and put sense into my intersections with the world, other subjects elbowed their way in—personalities, love, death and dying, faith, travel, and so on. And they began to vary in form: some showed up as straightforward autobiography; others leaned more toward vignette, personal essay, reverie, travelogue, and other kinds of account. To my surprise, a couple of poems popped up in the mix, and one stayed.

If you put them all together, they constitute a life's worth of episodes, a pretty full spread of me in the process of Getting There.

That's what lies ahead.

Tom Childers
Rehoboth Beach
2020

FOOD MIGRATIONS

1

Soup for Breakfast

I join Mom, Dad, and younger brother in upping the food ante over the years, till human limits keep it from going higher.

Around the 25th anniversary of my mother's death, I realized that my memory of her had dimmed, like an old photograph left in the sun. Afraid of losing the image altogether, I began trying to refresh it through writing, to rebuild the memories and make the picture of Mom whole again. It was uncannily like defragging a computer, gathering and reconstituting bits and pieces that had been scattered across the hard drive.

My best hope for recreating whole memories was to begin with the prominent and easily recalled and let these lead me to the buried records.

The strongest memory streams attached to Mom were her cooking and her emotional fragility (she had at least one nervous breakdown when I was very young). Cooking seemed by far the safer and less ambiguous theme. And since the subject was dear to her and has become dear to me, it was natural for Mom's cooking to take center stage.

My brother, Dick, and I formed our earliest food memories in Chillicothe, Ohio, where we moved when he was three and I was six and where we lived for twelve years. Mom came out of a German-American plain-cooking tradition. She had learned to cook from her mother, and I always felt that Mom had learned well—in contrast to her two sisters, who could hardly fry an egg between them. In Mom's early years as the household cook, she was hobbled by scope, by economy, and by inventory: by her plain-cooking tradition, by Dad's puny teacher's salary, and by a food supply that even for a small southern Ohio town in the forties and fifties seemed tediously ordinary.

Her cooking was further impaired by a husband who eschewed certain foods. A beef-poultry-and-potatoes farm boy, Dad grew up deeming rice and pasta tasteless no matter what they were sauced with, and pork, in all forms except pickled pig's ears, too greasy for human consumption. Dad was happy that things he didn't like found their way to the table only when he wasn't home for dinner.

From the start, Mom had a few memorable dishes at her command, such as left-over noodles sautéed in butter, salt, and pepper. That rich and simple dish derived directly from her German mother. But so did Mom's taste for vegetables plain (like Blue Lake green beans warmed up right out of the can) and overcooked (mushy Brussels sprouts and cabbage boiled to beige pudding), for dried-out dishes (desiccated fried calves liver, and bone-dry croquettes of chicken or canned salmon that no amount of lemon sauce could lubricate); and for stinting use of herbs and spices and outright rejection of garlic as too redolent of the scorned Italian immigrant neighbors of her childhood.

In time, perhaps responding to the maturing taste buds of her sons, but still operating within the template of Dad's preferences, she occasionally unveiled a new dish. Her refrigerator-Parker-House rolls were favorites of our family, all the more so because they were produced only for special occasions. And it came to be expected in May that she would find a dollar and send us to Betch's farm a block away to buy fresh asparagus, for cream-of-asparagus soup. (My brother confesses, "I knew it was superb, even though I wouldn't eat it.")

In a happy mood, Mom might approach the stove in her large-flowered apron and in a few mojo seconds produce a white sauce. With the sauce, Dick and I would love the over-cooked Brussels sprouts. (He remembers the sauce as eggy-buttery Hollandaise, and I think Mom called it that sometimes; but it wasn't, it was just a simple butter-flour-milk béchamel.)

Also, at any time of year—one hand in the flour bin, the other hand in the can of hydrogenated corn shortening (Spry)—she would throw together an outstanding pie—usually apple, sometimes peach or, during two particular weeks of June, sour cherries. The fruit didn't much matter, because the crust, flaky and creamy, made the pie delectable every time (just as, every time, when she extracted the first slice she would cry, "Oh darn, it's runny!") She made cakes, too, and good ones, but when she'd ask us what kind of cake we'd like for our birthdays, we always said, "Pie." Dick, with his birthday in June, could be more specific: "Sour cherry."

Unlike pie, fish was not a success. Her mother may never have taught her how to deal with it, but, dauntless, Mom made fish for dinner every Friday for years. This habit had nothing to do with her religion, she being Christian Scientist, or with the Catholic dietary laws of the day, she being strongly anti-Papist, or with the fish boats a-coming in on Friday, there being no fish boats in landlocked Chillicothe. I never did figure out why she chose Friday, but that's when she served fish, under the banner of salutary eating—usually a block of frozen haddock or halibut, baked or fried till it was as dry as a chip. (Years later, in the name of self-improvement, I spent a decade of my adult life studiously learning to like fish.)

Eventually, a steady source of inspiration caught her attention, in the form of ladies' magazines. Redbook, Ladies' Home Journal, and the like became her muse. They gave her new recipes or ideas on how to tweak her old standard concoctions and how to feed a family on a tight budget. New dishes began to show up on the table more frequently: hot dogs simmered in catsup; broiled open-faced hamburgers on bread, smeared with mustard; and a seven-layer casserole of rice, corn, tomatoes, hamburger, and three other layers that I can't remember. (Omigod; here they are on the Web, half a century later: green pepper, onion, and shredded cheese!). Leafing through one of her mags at age 11 or 12, I was jolted by a writer—obviously grasping for a publishable topic—insisting that soup would make a tasty and healthful way to start the day and expand the housewife's constrained and ultimately boring menu choices for breakfast. I passed the idea on to Mom, probably expecting nothing more than to shock her a little and perhaps reaffirm her traditions. Unflappable, she immediately put Campbell's condensed soups on the breakfast roster.

My brother recently sent me copies of some of Mom's recipe cards, bright yellow and chicken-shaped. Three of them held recipes for sour-cream coffee cake. The first time she made it, it became legend. Fifty years later, and Mom long gone, that cake is still the gold standard of our family's Christmas brunch. But no one can quite replicate it, as the ingredients on each card vary slightly. It is thought by certain cynical jokesters in our family, and our family is rife with them, that an unrecorded variation in the making of the cake gave Mom's version the edge. I am not that cynical.

In one ladies' magazine, Mom found a recipe that everyone else had missed. Tuna-noodle casserole was a sensation in the ladies-magazine world, and its universal solvent was Campbell's cream-of-mushroom soup. But Mom's recipe called for cream-of-tomato soup. It captivated everyone in the family, except my pasta-eschewing father, and immediately became a staple of the table whenever Dad was absent. Long after my diet and cooking turned haute cuisine, I would make it for myself, secretly, and eat almost the whole dish (serves four).

Our family had always eaten with gusto, greatly appreciating what we consumed, even if it was plain or ordinary, focusing now on the creaminess of the mashed potatoes, then on the amount of ketchup baked onto the meatloaf. As Mom's new cuisine started appearing, we began to eat more critically, with an eye to making future dining experiences pluperfect. Maybe Mom brought the family into her menu and recipe decisions, or maybe my brother, my father, and I wedged our way in. However it happened, food became participatory. Through the 50s, we—especially my brother and I—developed our critical powers and cheered her on to new heights of cooking. The first major participation I remember was convincing her to revoke the dietary law for Friday fish.

Mom seemed to thrive on our involvement and could be equanimous even when my brother lashed out in a moment of vile teenagedness, like rebuffing a soufflé she'd made just for him. I think, now, that as my brother and I got older and became increasingly busy with things that didn't involve her, like school, extracurricular activities, and social commitments, allowing us to participate in food was a strategy for holding onto us.

Not all of Mom's food forays succeeded. Sometimes she lacked the courage of her convictions and, just as a half-hearted flip of the skillet could land Julia Child's omelet half in the pan, half on the burner, Mom's dish could go awry. After my brother and I raved about Grandmother's green beans-cum-ham hock, Mom tried to reproduce it by boiling a single strip of bacon with a can of Blue Lake green beans. The outcome was insufficiently greasy, and listless.

Another time, a ladies' journal led Mom to beef Stroganoff. This was as exotic a recipe as our kitchen had ever seen, and the family trembled in anticipation. She assembled the beef strips, the herbs and spices, tomato paste, Worcestershire sauce, sour cream, mushrooms, onions, and other stuff, and the cooking began. It must have been a weekend, because I spent much of the afternoon in and out of the kitchen, watching the separately sautéed onions and mushrooms and garlic coalesce into a layered aroma. An interminable time later, the beef added its earthy tang, and dinner was ready. But Mom had made an executive decision. In the German enclave of her childhood Brooklyn, sour cream wasn't something one ate hot; one ate it cold, on potato pancakes. She decided to leave it out.

Dad, Dick, and I could barely contain our wonder as we sat down to the new dish. But Mom, taste buds to the rescue, took one bite and retrieved the sour cream from the refrigerator, and we each completed the dish for ourselves.

Dad's promotions at work started to show up in his paychecks, and the food budget expanded. When the family could rise above the cost of even Stroganoff beef, we might have steak or a standing rib, and it was always well done, as the cooking traditions on both sides of the family would have had it. But as the four of us lingered at the table for a debriefing, a consensus developed: Mom should cook the next roast only to medium-well. Over time, the post-prandial parley called for rarer and rarer still till, within a year, we were eating beef that was almost mooing.

The day I graduated from high school, we moved to Washington, DC, as Dad's career in federal prisons insisted. There, Mom's cooking could go into orbit. She discovered markets peddling the then extraordinary (wild boar, tortillas, lobster tails, fresh raspberries in February, exotic spices, and so on), made new friends with women who were similarly excited by new cooking ventures, and had more money to spend. Her food awakening continued; our dinner table had never supported such variety.

But now that her food journey was no longer impaired by finances or inspiration or food stock, Mom's personal impairments became clearer and more obviously in control. She was burdened with agoraphobia, in its most literal form: with all the marketing opportunities, it was difficult for her to exploit them, and only on her best, most confident days could she venture into the public eye of the marketplace. In Chillicothe, where grocery choices were few and unchanging, Dad could easily do the shopping, and usually did. But in DC, where choices were many and variable, shopping for other than the constantly ordinary was beyond his sensitivities. If Mom's cuisine were to continue to grow, the cook's—Mom's—decisions were needed, real-time, in the marketplace, but Mom's anxieties often kept her at home and out of the stores.

Her cuisine, once in a strong upward curve, hit a plateau. "I wonder what could have been, had the demons of depression and anxiety not weighed so heavily on her," my brother once mused. "Surely they never touched her refrigerator rolls." But the rise of our family table had come to a halt.

2

Trail Food

Backpacking with my brother on the Appalachian Trail in determined gourmet style.

When I was twelve or thirteen, I escaped the Boy Scouts. Fleeing not from the knot-tying or the accumulation of merit-badges, but from the mainstays of all-American boyhood: hiking and camping. But a paltry eight or nine years later, life squeezed me into a yellow VW Beetle with two other guys and a mountain of trail gear, and sent me hurtling toward five days of, what else?, hiking and camping.

* * *

Cub Scouts was comfortable. In uniforms of tranquil blue with yellow trim, we had wholesome fun, like making lanyards, playing games that were largely free of competition, and visiting cultural and civic sites. Mothers led "dens" of cubs, small coteries of young boys, and my own Mom was "den mother" of my den. Cub Scouting was about nourishing the woman-child bond, and we cubs cooperated whole-heartedly by holding fast to childhood.

When I graduated to the Boy Scouts in the fifth grade, I knew that growing up had commenced and life had taken a serious and threatening turn. The blue uniform became khaki. Den became

Troop. The agenda became citizenship, responsible behavior, service, and accomplishment. Bonding was about to shift from woman-child to man-child, which, peering out from behind a flower-print skirt, made me anxious.

Fortunately for me, the man who led our Boy Scout troop was not serious about much, nor threatening.

Boy Scout Troop Number Whatever had been a natural choice, since it met near my home and this new Tenderfoot could walk to meetings. We were a wimpy bunch of boys, but that fit me well, for I had no drive to achieve, Cub-wise. I persisted in scouts, Cub and Boy, because my parents expected me to. Later I figured out that they hadn't impressed my three-year-younger brother into scout service most likely because he was athletic and social. I was neither, so they opted for a scouting intervention.

Our troop didn't do much at the monthly meetings except review knots and deciduous trees, and the troop leader never seemed to exhort us to anything more ambitious than working for one or another merit badge that didn't require much investment of him or us. But since the first article of scouting was harmony with and subsistence in nature, facing off with the wild was essential. This meant walking through the wild (hiking) and living in the wild (camping). Thus, our leader—let me call him Phil—took us hiking and camping.

Two excursions stand out. On the first, a dozen of us were deep in the woods outside Chillicothe, Ohio at a large grey stone lodge. We were camping, which at this site meant keeping warm outdoors, making ones' own dinner, sleeping on the concrete floor of the lodge, and making one's own breakfast. Each scout laid and lit his campfire and cooked his dinner, the standard stew of hamburger, potatoes, carrots, onions, and water boiled in a coffee can. My potatoes and carrots didn't get cooked through, as usual, so I ate the onions and hamburger.

The lodge was one huge room with gargantuan fireplaces at either end. Being stone and shaded all day long, it was cold and damp. Most of us had flimsy hand-me-down sleeping bags; so when it came time to zip ourselves in, the idea of a fire on the hearth crystalized collectively, as did the realization that all those individual fires for all those individual dinners had stripped the near forest of its firewood and we'd have to forage further afield in the now dark, scary woods. Leader Phil, to the rescue, had spotted a heap of abandoned car tires behind an outbuilding. He threw them into the big fireplaces and lit them, and we got warm. The next day, when I walked into our living room coated in sticky, stinky black tire soot, Mom had a cow.

The second excursion found eight or ten of our troop walking through woods—hiking, it was called—up Mount Logan, a mountain east of town—a nice mountain, eminently hikeable. And historic in that on The Great Seal of the State of Ohio—designed when Chillicothe was the capital of Ohio—the sun shines promisingly on Mount Logan.

It would have been a fine hike except for two things. First, it was Saturday, and for me, physical activity was an unnatural way to spend a day off from school. Second, rain had been falling since early morning. We were a sullen, silent troop. By the time we were half a mile up Mount Logan, every seam in my clear-plastic raincoat had begun to leak and my shoes—no one in our troop had hiking boots—leaked and took on ooze from the trail. About noon, the rain stopped, and that brightened the mood a bit. Phil managed to get a fire going, as he had kept his matches dry somewhere in his unmentionables. We warmed ourselves before the blaze and tried to dry out. Most of us took our shoes off, poured the mud out of them, and propped them up in front of the fire. The soles of Phil's Hush Puppies caught fire. They stank, but not as bad as burning tires.

Eight or nine years galloped by. I was now 22 and fresh from the baccalaureate, living at home with Mom, Dad, and Dick for a few months before grad school. In late spring, Dick, bursting with athleticism, love of trees, and fancied lust for the wilderness, made a bold proposal: that he and I backpack on the Appalachian Trail, fifty miles in five days and, further, that we do it every summer and in time cover the whole Trail, Maine to Georgia.

I had been through scouting and knew the math: backpacking = hiking + camping. Dick's proposal resuscitated memories of tire smoke, bad food, and sodden shoes. And of physical exercise, which I had never willingly practiced. But the impressive negatives were tempered by an equal and opposite positive: that the proposal had been made at all, by my brother to me.

Dick, my sole sibling, was born three years after me. Consequently, he was always beginning things that I had gotten over or left behind, like training wheels, small bicycles and other toys, each and every classroom teacher, and ballroom dancing. But he never seemed to need protection or instruction by an older brother. He grew up fine without my tutelage, going his way while I went mine.

Truthfully, he did better in a couple of areas. I was a good student, but my hand-me-down teachers found him to be equally good. It was in things athletic and social that he exceeded me. He excelled in both. I was unathletic and a nerd. He celebrated the summer vacation; I celebrated going back to school in the fall. Through junior high and high school, the gulf between us widened.

During my junior year at the University of Maryland, I lived in a College Park rooming house with a few jock-y and not very academic classmates. In the rec room, they introduced me to beer as we watched television and, over time, accepted me. I started to develop a reasonably sociable personality and went so far as to ignore the racist and Christian underpinnings of fraternities in those days and pledged one of the premier fraternities, ATO, in the first semester of my senior year.

Dick, now a freshman at Maryland, must have been reassessing his older brother, for he pledged my fraternity that same year, as a freshman. A relationship seemed to be growing. So when presented with an otherwise repellant invitation to backpacking, I wasn't about to say no.

We asked my senior-year roomie to come along, in part because Barry was available and in part because he'd add flair to the proceedings. He was always ready with an interesting personal story or a joke. He was a bit of a clown of life. Studying in our little room, he would talk and he would joke and he would light his own farts with a match. Sometimes he burned himself. One weekend, he bet me that I couldn't drink an ounce of beer a minute for sixty minutes. We bought a cold case of Old Milwaukee, sat on our respective beds, and popped a shot every sixty seconds. I threw up after twelve shots; Barry, after fifteen. Some weekends Barry would go on a bender and end up somewhere he shouldn't, like Baltimore or downtown DC, without a nickel.

Backpacking's first tenet is to travel light. A tent wasn't necessary, as we'd be sleeping in lean-tos along the Trail. We bought a 12-ounce metal grill, a feather-weight collapsible wood saw, a tiny but powerful camp stove, and lighter-than-ordinary pots and pans, eating utensils, and canteens. So far, so good. But light, down-filled sleeping bags were too pricey, so we settled for the heavier cotton-and-kapok variety that we already had. Much of the requisite gear wasn't made in backpacking weight in those days, and still other gear never lent itself to light-weight versions. So we were stuck with the standard weight of ponchos, tarps, foul-weather gear, extra shoes, clothing, toiletries, hatchet, flashlights, folding shovel, first-aid kit, and so forth.

The second tenet of backpacking is roughing it. Trail food products of the day embodied that tenet. They hadn't yet reached beta-test stage. The stews were light, but they amounted to bagged bits of dehydrated vegetables and animal flesh which, on rehydration and heating, were hot and filling, period. Some trail products, like powdered eggs, bore an inverse resemblance to their fresh counterparts. However, being foodies, my brother and I weren't willing to rough it more than necessary: we wanted real food. So we amassed meat and poultry, canned and fresh vegetables, three dozen fresh eggs, fresh fruit, hard sausages, and some good cheeses. Tipping the scale were canned bacon for most breakfasts, at my brother's insistence, and wine for every dinner, at everyone's insistence.

On the morning of departure Dick, Barry, and I gathered in Mom and Dad's front hall. We divided the gear and food and packed it into three tall backpacks that I had picked up at the Army-Navy surplus store downtown. When bedrolls and ponchos got tied on top, the packs were nearly four feet tall. Barry stood a foot and a half taller than his pack.

He asked me, "Where's the snake-bite kit?"

"In my pack. Why?"

"'Cause we'll have to find it pronto when we get bitten," assuring me that copperheads would slip into our shoes and body-warm sleeping bags. I transferred the snake-bite kit to my front pocket.

We weighed our packs on the bathroom scale; they were about eighty pounds apiece. With the packs and the three of us crammed in, Mom and Dad's little yellow Beetle felt like a circus car overstuffed with clowns. As our smiling parents waved us off, I could feel my eyebrows raise and freeze—not superciliously, but surprisedly, dumfounded at what I was about to do and the fact that I of all people was the one who was going to do it.

We drove to a nearby entrance to the Appalachian Trail—probably close to the Maryland-Pennsylvania line, maybe Black Rock. Dick dropped off Barry, me, and the gear, drove fifty Appalachian Trail miles away to our destination, locked the car, and hitchhiked back.

And there we were, backpackers on the legendary AT.

For the whole five days, the weather was glorious, the mountain scenery was resplendent, and the trail was virtually deserted. The trekking invigorated body and soul. We hiked up mountains and down mountains, from valley to valley, through hemlock forests so dense they shut out the sun, across a mile of head-sized boulders that twisted our ankles at every step, under the arms of elegant elm woods, through acres of head-high rhododendrons, and across mountain prairies glistening with the crystals of morning dew. One night we slept on hemlock boughs that an environmentally incorrect hiker had lopped down the night before. We drank from mountain streams.

Our daily trek got us from starting place to lean-to in time to settle in before dark. After wrestling mountain terrain for nine or ten miles, dinner was inordinately prized. The first evening was Rock Cornish game hens—frozen when we left home, thawed by the time we stopped for the evening. Grilled over the wood fire, potatoes cooked in the coals, blanched green beans. White wine iced in the little spring next to us. Prideful gourmets in the wilderness.

The next morning we woke up in a chilly cloud bank and warmed our outsides by fire and our insides by three eggs each, canned bacon, and coffee, our standard breakfast. Midday, we took twenty minutes for fruit, cheese, and hard sausage. At our evening stopping place, dinner was half a chuck roast—cooked and frozen at home, thawing for two days en route, reheated over the fire. More fresh vegetables, probably peppers and zucchini sauté. Red wine.

After breakfast on the morning of day three, the benefit of eating cans of bacon and drinking copious amounts of wine came clear when we strapped into our backpacks: they were notably lighter, and the trail got easier because of it.

Breakfast and lunch were repeats of day two. Dinner was spaghetti with home-made tomato sauce, once frozen, augmented with the other half of the chuck roast. How we survived the unrefrigerated food, I don't know, but with fresh-grated Romano cheese, more sautéed green peppers, and a reasonable Chianti it tasted swell, and no one died.

Breakfast on day four was the standard eggs-bacon-coffee, but for lunch we were reduced to beef jerky and trail bars (in those days, chewy slabs of miscellaneous foodstuffs and chemicals tasting both slightly sweet and slightly bitter; today Atkins bars would be infinitely better). Dinner consisted of chips of dried carrots, onions, potatoes, beef, herbs, spices, and salt shaken out of a bag depicting smiley hiker faces in front of a blue sky. Add water, and heat to a gluttonous, tasteless glop. Not even a hefty dose of red wine made it food.

As planned, the eggs and canned bacon had been exhausted by day five, so we broke our fast with coffee and trail bars. Lunch was water and more trail bars. Dinner would have been another envelope of grim dried-food-product except that hallelujah! we were within spitting distance of our savior: the little yellow VW bug.

An hour and a half later, after showering at Mom and Dad's, we set about inhaling Mom's luxuriant dinner of meat, potatoes, vegetables, salad, and dessert—the details of it were unimportant—as we debriefed them about our backpacking adventures and detailed our gustatory victory over the trail.

* * *

Years later, that journey remains with me: long conversations with my brother—not the content, just the warming sense of dialogue—as we walked through forests, sat on rocks, shared a bottle of wine. Glorying in paths up and paths down, in the woods and mountain meadows. Growing used to those gigantic backpacks, which put some muscle definition into our thighs. Tracking the sometimes illusive trail together. Setting up camp and building fires in the evening and making meals.

Oddly, other than the preparations for the hike, no memory remains of Barry. Like his promised snake bites, he doesn't materialize in my recall. Shimmering personality to the contrary, I can't remember a comment, joke, fart, or other exhalation from him.

As if it had just been my brother and me, off on our own.

3

A Fish Story

Finding and losing the epitome of fish monger in southern Delaware.

John and I bought a second home in Rehoboth Beach in 1997. We immediately began scouting for foodstuffs, the way everyone does when they're setting up in a new place. For a lot of people, this amounts to where to buy cheap beef or raisin English muffins or eco-friendly paper towels. But for us, with nearly 30 years of Philadelphia's Italian and Reading Terminal markets under our belts—why are you staring at my waist?—Rehoboth looked like a wasteland: one ordinary supermarket after another, each sitting in its own hectare of stinking blacktop.

Cooking at our house had largely recovered from a ten-year bout of haute cuisine: home-made puff pastry, braised sweetbreads, snails poached in garlic butter, fish custards, meringues studded with toasted almonds, and so on. For the past decade and a half we had adopted a lighter continental and "American" improvisational style of cooking. And in a move to control our carbs, John's dessert and bread cookery had become rare. But we still ate and cooked seriously.

Six months into the food search in Rehoboth, word of mouth

led us to a cheese shop with a fine, if limited, line and an owner who was dogmatic about how his cheeses should be used (cooked vs. raw, savory vs. dessert, etc.); to a top-notch butcher, who often bought 4-H beef at auction and knew the steer by name; and to pretty good winter tomatoes and excellent summer produce at Bosie's stand. But our shopping basket had some gaping holes in it.

Bread, for instance, in southern Delaware was a lost cause; even in the best restaurants what they served was dreadful—undercooked, tasteless, or flabby, or all three—and no better when they made it in house. We brought our bread down from the Metropolitan Bakery in Philadelphia.

Seafood was another major hole. The chain supermarkets carried fish and shellfish—the standard kind you can find in the middle of Ohio, shipped in and looking weary and dry—farmed salmon, cod, haddock, shrimp, bags of mussels, flounder, cans of crab, jars of oysters, and so on. The few independent fish markets we found peddled the same fare, and some of it looked a bit fresher. Big demerits for a seaside town. Within earshot of the Atlantic surf, we expected a richer suite of briny victuals. Stuff that was still dripping the water it was taken from, still thrashing in the case.

One evening, a run-of-the-mill restaurant flabbergasted us with its sea scallops: bitey, deep-flavored sea-cylinders, not the faintly oceanic marshmallows that we were used to. We tracked down the chef, and he confessed, "The recipe is nothing, really; just pan-fried. It's where I get the scallops that makes the difference—Brown's."

The next day we visited Brown's Seafood.

We realized we'd been there a few months before. Brown's Seafood, on Route 1 just south of Rehoboth Beach, was a once-bright yellow, asphalt-shingled, two-story house on a concrete slab. Inside the torn screen door, the air was dank with uncertain moisture and the smell of a basement on the verge of mildew. The floor—the concrete slab—was wet and the color of dirt. The walls were streaky grey. A ragged piece of plywood covering a lobster tank was painted red and had tire tracks across one corner. You could easily take the place to be unsanitary—as we'd been warned by the wine merchant across the street—so we about-faced and walked out.

But on the second trip, starry-eyed in pursuit of good scallops, we saw it through a different lens. The walls and floor looked "authentic," the way a "real" fish store should look if it cared about product rather than presentation; and it smelled "authentic," of salt water, fresh-caught seafood, and hosed-down concrete.

Behind the display cases was a thin, brown-haired woman, mid-40s or 50, with a tan, handsome, furrowed face and a cigarette dangling from a corner of her mouth. Nearby was a stocky man of about 60, with a ruddy Irish complexion. He looked tired. A bloody apron covered the front of his red plaid flannel shirt and jeans. He was butchering a fish that must have been four feet long and two and a half feet wide.

The woman squinted through her smoke. "Hey fellas, what can I do for you?" Her lips barely moved, but the cigarette still bobbed up and down in the corner of her mouth, and the ash held tight.

"Do you have scallops?"

She jerked her head toward the far end of the fogged-over display case. "Yeah. Over there."

I asked for a pound. She picked them out one at a time, making sure they were whole and put them on a scale. The ash on the cigarette continued to grow as she leaned over what were soon to be our scallops.

We introduced ourselves. She said her name was Janet and pointed to the man: "That's Jim. He's the boss." He glanced at us, looked away, and grunted.

The cigarette got properly flicked, the scallops got wrapped, the bill got paid, and we said, "Goodbye, Janet; goodbye, Mr. Brown." He brusquely corrected us: he was Yuengling, not Brown. Brown was the name of the owner 30 or so years ago, and he, Yuengling, had never bothered to change the name of the store.

That evening, I coated the scallops top and bottom with corn meal and sautéed them in a red-hot skillet. They tasted even better than the ones at the restaurant.

The next day, I went looking for something else. Yuengling was standing behind the counter, doing nothing. He still looked tired—but it could have been boredom. I asked why his scallops had so much flavor. His eyes lit up and his mouth moved with a purpose, as if he were gearing up to say something important. "You gotta know how to buy them," he said. "I get them as soon as the boat docks, from the top of the load, the last ones they brought up." He lectured about how scallop boats used to stay at sea for many days, but were now required to dock sooner, and how the scallops were fresher; and about how he shucked his own scallops and didn't wash them, so they retained their natural strong flavor. This is what "dry" scallops are—unwashed.

Yuengling dealt with seasonal seafood. He got most of it from local fishermen and imported a small percentage of it fresh from other US waters. The only thing he bought frozen was shrimp. He didn't carry the standard line of seafood, so there was never much in the case; but what was there was of the season.

One day he was filleting flounder—a fish that had never been a favorite of mine in restaurants because it was invariably mushy and bland. I brought two of them home, along with more of the redoubtable scallops. On each sautéed flounder fillet I laid a few scallop quenelles (dumplings) and painted them with a paprika-to-mato-cream blush sauce. Full-flavored flounder, rich quenelles.

We walked in on Yuengling later that month and found him standing behind the case in red flannel shirt uniform, doing nothing. "What do you birds want?" he blurted. It turned out that what I wanted was lying in the case. "Ooh," sez I, "skate." It had been over 15 years since I'd seen skate wings, in a fish-slimed storefront in Philadelphia's Italian Market.

Yuengling sold me the two he had, culls from the nets of a local fisherman. Their fate was to be fried in brown butter and paired up with braised cabbage. But our long-term passion for the dish was unrequited, as Yuengling's supply of skate was limited. Then one day Janet said, "Jim had me freeze the last ones that came in, for 'the two guys from Philadelphia'." That would be us. We were hooked. We were in Jim's inner circle. Over time he provided major ingredients for the kitchen and major tutorials about them.

He usually looked worn out—unanimated—unless we had a question about seafood or fishing. Even animated, he was gruff. He scoffed when we opined that Chesapeake Bay oysters were deadly and explained that the beds in the Bay were inspected more frequently than anywhere else. He shucked his own and left them in their liquor. They were all you could want in oysters on the half-shell or, with wild mushrooms and cream, the only surf and turf that makes sense to me: a gratin that tastes of ocean floor and forest floor all at once.

One day I watched him butcher a gigantic halibut. Every time I'd tried halibut in a restaurant—even good ones—it had been dry, and I thought that was its natural state. But I bought some anyhow, and I learned immediately that the restaurants overcooked it. With a few minute's hot baking under parchment, the halibut filet turned into a mousse, moist and light, like a custard. (I still can't figure why that custardy outcome happened just that once. No matter how long or short I cook it or at what temperature, whether I cover it, whether I moisten it, my subsequent halibut dishes have retained the texture of sinew—delicious, but not a pudding.)

Another day, Jim introduced us to tuna bellies—fatty, full-flavored, and succulent. No wonder they're used for sashimi.

One overcast November day Jim's capstone item was sitting in the case: greenish-grey flat blobs about the size of small frisbees. They looked like organ tissue and, in fact, were: monkfish liver. What the hell do you do with that? Jim said oven-poach it and serve at room temperature with a wasabi-soy sauce. It came out like a fish-flavored foie gras—a spectacular hors d'oeuvre that some of our friends actually liked and that everyone discussed ("Fascinating," "Fabulous," "Eeyew," and so on).

Then there were blue-fish cheeks and grouper cheeks and numerous local fishes, some of which Jim caught on his days off. He also sold a few prepared foods. The crab cakes were too bready, but the freshly smoked tuna was his justifiable pride and joy. Warm from the smoker, it carried the dark seafood taste of canned tuna, but with a fresh, smoky dimension.

So it went at Brown's. Passionate cooks cook from the market—from what's rare, or unusually fresh, or locally seasonal, or even beautiful. (Think of a huge cauliflower ringed with dark green leaves that insists on being a centerpiece on your table for a couple of days before you turn it into food.) You work from the ingredient, cooking by serendipity and reveling in the invention that that demands. Jim Yuengling peddled serendipity in seafood—the chance ingredients that breathe excitement into making dinner.

But after only a couple of years of our devoted custom, cook's nightmare #1 descended. At 62, Jim Yuengling succumbed to the aches and pains of decades of handling sea-borne products. When New Year's week, 2003, ended, the lights at Brown's Seafood went out for the last time.

4

If I Should Die Before I Eat

Going out on a gustatory high note.

Craig Claiborne, the legendary *New York Times* food critic and cookbook author, may or may not have been contemplating his own mortality when he ordered his dream meal in Paris in 1975. Bankrolled by American Express in a promotional gambit, he sampled 31 dishes of the highest of high-cuisine food and many rare wines over the course of five hours. The extravagance of the feast and its $4,000-bill (about $190,000 in 2020) caused an uproar inside and outside food circles, including Pope Paul VI's public cry of "scandalous." It wasn't Claiborne's last supper. But he did die, 25 years later, of causes unrelated to gustatory indulgences.

When Ruth Malloy, a local poet and historian of West Philadelphia, invited the whole neighborhood to her 90th birthday party, she made a point that the community was throwing the party for her. The invitation was ambiguous as to the amount or nature of food, or the kind of entertainment; but it was unambiguous on the weather, noting that it was sure to rain. "But," Ruth assured us, "there will be cake." Actually, she had to go to the emergency room the morning of the party and missed it. She died two years later.

Tucker Bobst, from whom we purchased our Philadelphia

house, was a surrealist artist. When we bought the house, the sticker shock was so great we thought, what the hell, we might as well add in a couple of Tucker's own works. One is a large painting of Baryshnikov. The other is an antique pencil box painted to look like the glazed green tiles you find in subways. The tiles are pierced by a few trompe-l'oeil bullet holes with little coronas of blood. Across the top of the tiles, painted in Times Roman Shadow, is written "Cuisine Terminale," a pun on the Reading Terminal Market in downtown Philadelphia and the bullet- and blood-riddled corpse of the pencil box. Death by food.

In 2004, the Philadelphia Inquirer detailed the last meals of a sample of convicts put to death since January 2003. Some refused any sort of meal. Not surprising. Although few things can take my mind off food, imminent death, especially my own, probably would. But most of the prisoners ate. The most high-toned item listed was a bottle of Dom Perignon, which was denied, on account of the liquor-free policy of the prison.

Food captured me long ago not for its comfort, though that must have been part of the allure; not for showing off in the kitchen, although I admit to doing that from time to time; not for ministering to those I love, even though that's a major reason I cook; but for the way ingredients come together to make a dish, and a progression of dishes a menu—all of which act on the palate at the instant of consuming, or on the palate's memory over the course of a meal.

If I am ever forced to think of terminating this food journey, I assume it will be against my will and on my way to nothingness. And if I'm given a reprieve long enough to have something to eat before I enter the void, I'm also going to assume the tastebuds are intact and the body is reasonably vigorous, that my dining companions can enjoy the food with me, and that only I know that this is my last meal, so as not to dampen the festivity.

I rarely envision my own mortality, but when I do, I sometimes imagine my last act to be playing squash with some unknown person, the racquet in my right hand and a dry martini, straight up with two olives, in my left. I don't know how to bring this off, since it's hard to take a sip and get the ball into the "sweet spot" of the racket at the same time. Actually, I can hardly achieve the latter even without gin.

My more realistic dream of terminal eating is bifurcated. In the first scenario, a noted chef walks out of a prestigious kitchen—think Thomas Keller of the French Laundry—and insists that I submit to the chef's tasting menu. I had a similar experience at the Red Cat Cafe on Martha's Vineyard years ago, when Bill Clinton was in the White House and the night after the Clintons dined there. We ordered the chef's menu but were denied information on its courses till they were set before us. Now *there's* an exciting food evening! And for about one-fortieth of Craig Claiborne's feast.

In the second scenario I conjure a menu of my own. The architecture is small-plate. Of course, I have my loved ones around, wrapped in total pre-appreciation of every bite they're about to take and solid confidence in my omniscience in selecting food and drink. The dishes will include, unless I run across something more delectable between now and then: a dozen gigamotto oysters on the half-shell with a glass of iced gin; baked foie gras and Banyuls Sauterne; asparagus-leek "veloute" (Patricia Wells' *Paris Cookbook*); a small portion of fresh sea urchin on velveteen potato puree with a dash of curry powder (a la Gramercy Tavern in New York); salade Lyonnaise—frisée, lardons, and sautéed potato cubes, capped with a poached egg; sweetbreads sous cloche—crisp-fried sweetbreads on lean bacon on an English muffin, napped with a light bechamel and served under a glass bell (Time-Life cookbooks); zucchini tian, a gratin of green squash, rice, milk, and garlic; Humbolt fog, Vacherin Mont d'Or, Abbaye de Belloq sheep cheese and Riviera pear; and warm chocolate soufflé

Then an espresso doppio, and take me Jesus!!

FOOTINGS

5

Reverberations from Childhood

Sounds that linger from a small Midwestern town.

Under the still glowing dark blue bonnet of a summer sky,
soprano calls of neighborhood kid to neighborhood kid
hiding from streetlights
in sharp shadows found behind garages and under bushes,
playing almost-muted tag
and hide-and-seek
till we were hollered in for bed.

* * *

Vegetable rustlings as neighbor urchins burrow through a field
of father-high asparagus ferns
forging rooms and forts—
new worlds in the mid-day heat.

* * *

Wood thwocks wood in our back yard.
Mr. Dixon, our neighbor, joins Dad, my brother,
    and me in croquet and
assorted exclamations of victory and defeat.

* * *

Small, crescendoing Oo-oo-oos.
Mom races out of the house,
  Oos trailing behind her in speech balloons,
to catch our Plymouth rolling slowly
down the driveway
while eight-year-old me tries to reset the hand brake
  that I'd playfully released.
I had never seen Mom run and scream at the same time.

* * *

Breath, sharp intake, by him, by me.
Penknife stuck in my little brother's six-year-old thigh.
Mumblety-peg: dexterous wieldings of a pocket knife
to stick upright in the ground.
My "spank-the-baby" flip gone awry.

* * *

Stifled sobs when the furry black howler to my violin practice,
  Tippy the dog, dies.
Comes home and coughs up blood and is gone before dinner,
Mom and me with him on the linoleum floor.
Found some rat poison, Dad surmised.

* * *

Hollow silence when snow covers everything on our block,
the world holding its breath
pierced now and then by the splat of a slush ball
  nailing some kid's hat.

* * *

Fleshy thuds of me pummeling my bully nemesis
  in the yard next door
amazing multitudes of neighbors
spying through their venetian blinds.
Amazing me even more.

* * *

Sweet airs in our small living room
Dad at the violin or piano
A 45-rpm record player cranking out popular tunes
Mom humming modest soprano mmmms from the kitchen.

* * *

Flat, undistinguishable talk sounds, gargly murmurs
spilling out of my friend, HR's, window on ghostly
   grey-white light, down to me
rooted to the sidewalk.

Television.

Eventually, in HR's living room, the most vivid noise imaginable:
   Howdy Doody, Captain Video, Flash Gordon.

Years before my family even thought of having a TV
HR's folks led the pack.
And with color, too:
plastic panel fastened to the screen—blue at top, green at bottom,
   pink-flesh colored in between
as if every image was going to be Caucasians doing something
   on grass under a clear sky.

6

A Touch of Country

Caught twixt hillbilly roots and city life.

My brother recently sent me a photograph of our father. It was probably taken in the early thirties. Dad was 16 or 17, wearing coveralls and a straw barn hat pushed to the back of his head and holding a calf in his arms, casually, for no other reason than that he could. He looks strong, handsome, freckled, fresh, and at one with his farm-boy circumstance.

The at-oneness is an illusion. He was growing up on a small farm in southern Ohio—165 acres that was more rock fields and scraggly forests than arable land. With hard work, it sustained his mother, father, sister, and him, but with the vicissitudes of weather, the return on investment was unpredictable. Chores began at four a.m. and lasted till suppertime and beyond, and there was no day off. His father, and eventually he, plowed with horses. There was never indoor plumbing; electricity and a tractor arrived only after Dad had left the farm for good.

And he was determined to leave. Fortunately, he was born to people who preferred their children educated, no matter what career they chose, and who lived near Rio Grande, Ohio, a one-horse village that happened to have a teacher's college. And that was

Dad's escape route. Over the ten years following the date of that photograph, he met and wed my mother, started his work on a BA in education, got a teaching job in Chillicothe, completed the BA, and escaped the farm.

But there was something else to leave behind.

Dad descended directly and recently from hillbillies, through his mother. (It was a coincidence that he was called Billy as a kid.) I have a photograph of the 19th-century one-room log cabin where his grandfather was born; and another picture of that grandfather, astride a mule, a snow-white beard to his waist, a slouch hat shading his eyes. True to the hillbilly demographic, my Great-grandfather White and his family were very poor, minimally educated or not at all, and eking out life on probably a small parcel of land in the remote back county.

The lot of Great-grandfather White's children—Dad's mother and her siblings—had improved, if not greatly. They were well-mannered and civil and spoke without a country accent. Notwithstanding a hickish reminder or two—my grandmother's diary refers to my father not as Billy, but as Boy—she, her brother, and two sisters had shaken off a lot of the hill dust of their forbearers and were fairly gentrified. The two who married married up, to a town-dweller and a farmer close to town.

Dad held affectionately onto his farming past once it was truly past, by visiting his relatives on their farms frequently and planting a garden in the city. But he continued to be embarrassed by or repelled by the hill folk dangling from nearby branches of the family tree. It took one last family reunion for him to shake himself out of that tree.

When I was growing up, the Childerses of Granddaddy's side and the Whites of Grandmother's side gathered for a family reunion each summer in a park with thirty or forty relatives. Mom, Dad, Dick, and I would drive south about 50 miles to Skunk Hollow or Raccoon Creek or some other public park. I didn't know the names of three quarters of the people. Perhaps mirroring my father's attitude, I couldn't uncover any common interests between them and me with which to fuel a conversation. On top of that, the sole reunion entertainment for the boys was baseball, which I not only didn't play well, but abhorred. I would read a book, even though—maybe because—I knew it was anti-social. When I tired of that I focused on food: four or five picnic tables weighed down with dishes from everyone's kitchens. So what if there was too much yellow mustard in Aunt Fanny's potato salad? So what if someone's eternal lemon Jell-O with shredded carrots was as bland as an oak chip? There was plenty of other, better stuff. I entertained myself by carefully loading my thin paper plate so the fried chicken, potato salad, pickles, spiced peaches, green bean casserole, ambrosia salad, and meatloaf didn't flow together into a tutti-frutti glop or, worse, soften the plate and make it collapse in my lap.

Dad had always felt that we should make an appearance. But with an anti-social streak greater than mine, he was always ready to depart as soon as he arrived, and we were heading home after a couple of hours. Happily, the barely known great aunts and second cousins twice removed didn't have much time to ask me what grade I was in now or why I didn't want to play baseball.

I don't remember how many reunions Mom, Dad, Dick, and I attended, but I remember the last one. I was probably nine or ten. Everything was proceeding normally: there was chatter and baseball (a book for me); and, as soon as someone in charge deemed that enough food had arrived, the platters and bowls were laid out and everyone advanced on the trough. I don't know where the rest of my immediate family was, but I had filled my plate and was ready to dig in when a late-20s beat-up black sedan pulled up near the crowd. I had never seen the car before. Like clowns out of a telephone booth, thirteen adults, children, and infants popped out. I had never seen them before, but they were known to others. They talked with a strong southern twang. Many teeth were missing. They were dressed funny—mismatched patterns, dirty shoes, no shoes, pants too short, pants too long, slips hanging below dresses.

41

But they weren't clowns; they were kin. One had a guitar.

After hellos, they joined everyone at the buffet, and when the eating ceased, they huddled round the man with the guitar and began twanging out country songs. In those days, before country music had mainstreamed, my mother, father, brother, and I were unanimous on at least one point: detestation of country (hillbilly) music. Not many minutes later Dad hustled us into the car, and we left these and all other hill cousins in our dust, forever more.

But even with the yoke of yokels off his neck, Dad was still a farm boy. When Mom and Dad thought it would be a growth experience for me to take an excursion on my own, they chose Grandmother and Granddaddy's farm. One summer morning Mom packed my bags and me into Sadie, our 1939 black Plymouth sedan, and made me promise to practice the piano every day. I was eleven.

Dad drove me, 75 minutes door to door. This wasn't going to be like the carefree Sunday day trips with my family. On such a Sunday, Dad would sometimes let me ride Sadie's running board all the way up the drive to the farmhouse. Today I sat in the passenger seat, demure and nervous, as we bounced along the stony ruts to my big rendezvous with free will and self-control.

We passed Grandmother's vegetable garden on the left and an untended meadow on the right. Through billows of road dust the rear-view mirror reflected a field with boulders and trees, where we almost never went except to hunt squirrels when I got older. Up front, at the top of the hill were the house—white clapboard—and, in grey weathered wood, a barn, coal shed, pig sty, smoke house, hen house, tool house, corn crib, and two-seater outhouse. The farmhouse needed paint, the wire fence around the house was rusted, and the barn listed to the left. And it was all beautiful, because I knew that beyond the buildings was a sometimes green, sometimes golden plateau where corn or tobacco were raised; and beyond that, my favorite landscape: a sloping valley with pastureland in the foreground, a large stand of young woods below that, and a small creek at the bottom.

After Dad left, I spent the rest of the day revisiting the farm. Everything seemed new on this trip, or magnified. On our regular Sunday day trips, I would wander the grounds and poke into the barn and other outbuildings, but there was only enough time for a sampling. Now, with a week ahead of me, time slowed down and the focus of things sharpened: the hay, more scented; the pig sty, more pungent; the chickens, goofier; the pump water, cooler and crisper; the grapes on the arbor above the pump, deeper purple.

I don't remember dinner, but afterwards we sat in the dining room by a large glass kerosene lamp. To the hollow tick of the mantel clock, Granddaddy and I read, and Grandmother picked thread out of an old dress to re-use on a new one. Bedtime came sooner than I expected, since the rooster was the alarm clock, and he was set for daybreak. Grandmother walked me up two narrow flights to my bedroom under the eaves with a straw-filled mattress and flour-sack sheets and tucked me in. They slept downstairs off the living room.

The clock struck the hour and half-hour and quarter-hour and three-quarter-hour, bonging up the stairwell to my room. Night sounds unknown to a city boy poured in through the open window—insects; animals chattering and mating and eating each other; branches rasping against the eaves. I slept fitfully. At some point the sound of the clock became a skeleton walking toward me down a railroad track on footless ankles that went tock, tock, tock.

Dawn eventually arrived and I heard the sounds of breakfast downstairs. Later, I helped with a few chores, but was too small or too untrained in the work of the farm to contribute much. After lunch I explored the barnyard and the hayloft and eventually came inside to face my covenant with Mom. That there was no piano was no excuse. In the living room, under a painting of red and white roses with a rip in one corner, stood the ages-old pump organ that my father had learned on.

There at the organ, on probably my third day on the farm, I started feeling odd—a queasy stomach, a bit of a fever. Grandmother diagnosed me and called Mom and Dad. They pronounced it homesickness. I had nothing to say in the matter, but I thought it preposterous that one could get physically ill just by being away from home. Dad came and got me the next morning.

Next year, we tried again. This time it was two of us—my kid brother, Dick, and me. If I was twelve, he was nine. Mom, always worried lest we be a burden on Grandmother, made us swear that we'd be absolutely no trouble at all. We swore. Practicing piano on the pump organ wasn't an issue this year, as I had been sacked by my piano teacher for negligence.

The whole family drove down one summer Sunday for noon dinner. In mid-chew I remembered the chicks my brother and I had gotten for Easter—one pink, one green—and had donated to Grandmother when they got too big for the city. I asked how Bert and Ernie (I don't remember their real names) were doing. Grandmother said, "They turned out to be the meanest little banty roosters. Had to cull them." She pointed at the platter in the middle of the table. "But they're pretty tasty." So they were.

Mom and Dad drove back home, leaving Dick and me with our vows of good behavior. Except for a couple of faux-pas—like when Grandmother's Baptist ears couldn't stand hearing us say "darn" once more, and she told us so; and when I informed her that crushing Saltines in one's soup wasn't good manners, after she'd just done it—we were good. Dick and I didn't argue with or antagonize each other—which was surprising, since we were never out of one another's company—and we didn't aggravate our grandparents.

Our list of daily chores—hauling a few buckets of water, feeding the chickens, or churning butter—was quickly exhausted. We spent the rest of the daylight hours exploring the nooks and crannies of the barn and outbuildings and staying away from the gigantic scary hog in the pig sty. We played checkers with Grandmother or each other, tried to tame the feral cats that lived under the house, and fooled around on the rusted-out hulk of a Model T in the side yard.

Several times we walked down the road to see Great Uncle

Lewis, Grandmother's bachelor farmer brother, and his beagle. He might give us lunch. A couple of times we walked him up the hill to Grandmother's for dinner. A couple of days we rode into town with Granddaddy to pick up supplies at the general store—chicken feed, nails, pipe tobacco for Uncle Lewis, a pair of socks, and so on—and a bottle of Nehi orange soda dripping with ice water.

We picked elderberries for a pie and harvested vegetables from the kitchen garden and helped prepare some of them for dinner. One morning we went with Grandmother to gather eggs and one evening, with Granddaddy, to watch him milk the cow. We watched Grandmother scatter corn in front of the chickens and wait till one got close enough to grab for dinner.

We walked down the back valley and splashed in the creek and built a dam to trap minnows. Under the monster apple tree in the front yard we sharpened a couple of long sticks, jabbed them into the fallen apples, and flung the apples over the fence. We captured jars of lightning bugs in the evening.

One morning, armed with yards of binder twine and a dull, rusty hatchet, we set off across the cow pasture and into the valley. We found two saplings growing next to a small bluff. We chopped them off about three feet from the ground, placed the severed branches from bluff to trunk, secured them with twine, and covered the construction with more leafy branches. We brought lunch down from the house and sat inside our little haven till dinner time. The next day we returned, to find the leafy bower in ruins. There was a telltale cow plop beside it: the cows had probably used our bower to scratch their big rumps.

Then the folks came to get us, and the week was over. Dick and I returned the next year and the next for another and another of what we later agreed were the sweetest weeks of our childhoods.

There were other times when we stayed a few nights with Dad's sister and her family, on a farm near Grandmother and Granddaddy—a more prosperous farm, with an outhouse, to be sure, but with a pump at the kitchen sink and a whole room that, by adding a galvanized tub on Saturday evening, became a bathroom. I spent days one August walking a parched hillside, helping my cousin Ray load bales of hay that weighed as much as I did. I witnessed procreation among the sheep. I helped Aunt Evelyn put up peaches and pickles—one quart of each for every day of the year.

Despite some time for private meandering and a handful of planned entertainments, like attending a square dance where my uncle was the caller, or taking in a slapstick hillbilly film (Homer and Jethro), my aunt and uncle's farm was edging close to agri-business—gigantic corrugated metal chicken coops, herds of sheep and cattle, monstrous farm machinery, many acres of cultivated crops. This didn't interest me, and generic, foggy memories are the only residue.

The endearing, enduring moments happened at Grandmother's and Granddaddy's, on the farm where Dad was raised to be the farm boy he could never quite leave behind. This was where my brother and I stored up durable, sparkling memories of rolling acreage, the simplicity of subsistence, and the poetry of living close to the land. For several days or a week, absolutely certain that I would return safely to my own home, I could revel in that country realm, and still remain a city boy, with perhaps just a touch of country.

7

On My Mother's Side

Grandpa's nine-year enigma.

In the spring of 1943, my mother took a train from West Virginia to Buffalo with three-year-old me and my newborn brother, Dickie, so she could introduce him to her side of the family, Grandma and Grandpa Kohlrusch.

The train ride was probably an overnighter. Surprisingly, I wasn't excited enough to remember it. The only thing I recall from the whole trip was when Grandma took me to a fairground on the edge of Lake Erie. We were waiting to see a man get shot from a cannon, and I was standing behind Grandma, facing the back of her skirt. Somehow I lost track of the fact that it was Grandma and wandered away to look for her. Two officers found me and fed me ice cream as I cried, till I saw the striped ribbon on Grandma's straw boater floating toward us through the crowd.

About two years later, the three of us visited again—this time, in Cleveland, where Grandma and Grandpa had moved, to a little white house on Euclid Avenue. The back yard was large, and Grandpa's rose garden took up the whole space. I trailed after Mom and Grandma, face-level with the flowers, absorbing the big sweet scent and the big pastel globes. I knew the garden was impressive when Grandma said that Grandpa's brother, my great uncle, who still lived in Germany, was renowned for his rose garden. I was elated to have living relatives in another land, but I was confused that my country was at war with them—but it must not have mattered, since none of the adults mentioned it.

By the time of this trip, my food focus had grown, and some of Grandma's cooking began to register, especially the omelet filled with grape jelly and the noodles fried in butter. We also had the food of Grandma's neighbor lady one day, a lunch of macaroni salad—really good, my first exposure to real mayonnaise in lieu of Miracle Whip. But the house had a strange odor that I remember to this day, like soured milk mixed with a cleaning solution. I didn't mention the smell to Mom or Grandma.

In another few years, when I was nine or ten, Mom's parents had moved yet again. I don't know if it was the itinerant nature of Grandpa's tool-and-die profession, or the itinerant nature of Grandpa, or something else, but they moved a lot—in Ohio: Toledo, Canton, Cleveland, and Springfield; and Brooklyn, San Diego, and St. Petersburg. Those are the ones I know of, and there may have been more.

This visit, it was Springfield. Dad wasn't particularly drawn to his in-laws, and the demands of work back at home, in Chillicothe, was his excuse for not staying over. He drove Mom, Dick, and me to the new house, about an hour and a half. Our dog had become afraid of riding in the car and spent the time panting nervously. She flinched whenever we drove under the arches of a bridge. I don't remember if we had to let her out to pee on the way; but we boys could always depend on a little blue plastic bottle with a handle and a screw top if we felt the call. After we unloaded at Grandma and Grandpa's—a white house, like the one in Cleveland, but larger—and everyone exchanged hellos, Dad and the dog drove back home. He would return in a week to collect us.

Since we stayed longer on this visit than earlier ones, more of Grandma made its mark on me: her gentle, generous personality, her industrious nature, her "bad legs" (varicose veins?), her sensible Red Cross shoes, the way her Brooklyn accent twisted "earl" into "oil" and "oil" into "earl." I noted that my sweet, gentle grandmother chased cats out of the shrubberies with a broom. Maybe that's where Mom got her distaste for cats.

Her cooking made stronger impressions on this trip: warm, crusty homemade bread; pancakes made from fresh-grated potato, with apple sauce; a coarse apple kuchen that I knew only my German Grandma could make, until I learned that it came from the side of a Bisquick box; cocoa nectar ("necta" if you're from Brooklyn), a tall glass of coffee, chocolate, and ice cream; and Vernor's ginger ale float with vanilla ice cream. She made these things for my brother and me, and only for us, we were sure.

As time went on, she often came to our home to visit, by herself, especially when Mom was feeling the strongest pull of her anxieties, to help out around the house and offer some mother-daughter therapy. She made dishes that Dick and I favored, she dealt with us gently, and we loved her.

Grandpa was another story.

He was a short man, but I didn't realize how short till I was into my teens, and taller. But he was also stern of demeanor, large of stomach, and Germanic of accent—in a word, fearsome to a kid. And his status as a Mason—with the trappings of crimson fez and sash, and ceremonial sword, and the mysteries of Masonry—rendered him exotic, as well. I was awed and afraid. Within the limits of polite behavior, I avoided contact.

As I grew older, taller, and more confident, Grandpa faded into the background. He had turned into—or I had turned him into—a transparent man, background noise. Eventually I noticed that grown-ups in our family treated him that way. The eldest daughter, Aunt Helen, had subtracted herself from the family equation years ago by eloping with a handsome alcoholic. The remaining sisters, now grown—Mom and Aunt Alfreda—interacted with Grandpa almost formally, in monosyllabic exchanges. They didn't seem to have much to say to him, or he to them.

Grandpa acted like the master of the house, but Grandma treated him like a visitor who was about to overstay his welcome. Their conversations were unspirited and functional—about shopping, unclogging the sink, setting a time for dinner. Conversations that might engage other couples, like discussing the evening news, commenting on letters from friends and relatives, sharing the Sunday funnies, or gossiping about neighbors, didn't happen in my hearing. I did overhear Grandma complaining about him to Mom and Aunt Alfreda. Among other things, she resented the dems, dats, dohs, and mits of his heavy German accent, especially after so many years on English-speaking soil. They slept in twin beds.

I couldn't figure out why Grandma catered to him in the kitchen. She cooked his breakfast to order and served him iced coffee when he came home for lunch. She made corned beef and cabbage often, because he loved it. And potato dumplings, and sticky buns. Food seemed to be the sole detente in the cold war of their lives. At Thanksgiving, or whenever we had roast turkey, Grandma carved the bird in the kitchen and brought the heaping platter to the table. Then she returned to the kitchen and came back bearing another platter with the turkey carcass, which she set in front of Grandpa. He ate the tail first, then dove in with both hands, gnawing and sucking on every little bone, oblivious to the rest of us dining more decorously with knife and fork.

I blamed my grandfather for Grandma and Grandpa's stand-off, laying it to Grandpa's aloof and cool nature, which triggered a chill reciprocity from Grandma. As it turned out, I had lit on the wrong reason. When I was grown, I learned from my cousin Carol that in the early 1920s, Grandpa had run off with another woman, leaving Grandma with three young girls.

She grubbed to make ends meet. She manufactured chocolates and fondants on a marble slab in their little apartment and took in laundry. At one point, she opened a tearoom in Brooklyn, where she turned out delectable pastries—which I know, because she later reproduced some for me. Unfortunately, the opening of the shop coincided with the stock market crash of 1929, and it closed after a short run. Grandpa returned soon thereafter, tail between his legs, and asked Grandma to take him back. Desperate for the girls' welfare, she did.

Grandma and he moved one last time, after Grandpa retired from his tool-and-die trade, to a tiny white cinder-block house in St. Petersburg, Florida. Periodically we drove down from the north and stayed with them for four or five nights.

By then, Grandpa seemed to take more interest in the family. Maybe he had relaxed. He never went to the beach with us—where we spent the bulk of our time—but we did some gardening together, and he played many lively rounds of pinochle every evening with my father, my brother, and me. He and I grew closer, at least when we were in each other's presence. Never to the point of a hug; but there were shared jokes and laughs and even some discussions of politics and social affairs and the like. For the first time, he felt like family, rather than the invisible grandfather. Enough so that I almost didn't remember how he monopolized the Thanksgiving carcass or how he forsook Grandma and his daughters.

8

Daisy's Diary

Grandmother's year and a half of diary-keeping reveals more than the word count would suggest.

About five years ago, decades after Grandmother died, my brother mailed me a copy of her diary. It had been held by Aunt Evelyn, Dad's sister, and partially annotated by her children. Those grey photocopies of thirty-six pages, in a saddle-stitched 6 ½-by-8-inch ruled notebook, held pencil-writ entries that were often no more than a single word, and it challenged the social scientist in me to see what mysteries lurked there.

* * *

As a kid, I knew my father's parents led a life different from ours. After all, my family and I lived in a city, they lived on a farm. Grandmother cooked on a wood stove. In the field, Granddaddy plowed up the red clay behind Bert and the other horse whose name I can't recall.

My life was different there, too. I peed out back of the woodshed or did number two in the outhouse where toilet paper was, at best, the Sears catalog and butt-jumping spiders were doubtless lurking under the toilet seat. I tried to tame the cats living under the house. I helped with various farm chores.

It was another way of living, but only just, and I thought at the time that when I was on the farm I belonged there, that I was a genuine city-country half-breed. After all, I was related directly to a farmer father, farmer aunt, farmer uncle, and farmer grandparents, I knew one animal from another, and I did some actual farm work.

At age 64, with the diary in front of me, I realized that I comprehended their way of living only vaguely, through the veiled senses of a child who treated the farm not as a secondary home, but a theme park. Compounding my muzzy perspective was the fact that contact with my grandparents was almost invariably on their day of "rest," Sunday, when the only work allowed by country Baptist traditions was the necessaries to keep man and beast alive, or at family reunions, where they did no work at all.

On top of that, the contacts weren't many—perhaps six or eight a year. There was no space for quality interactions between child and grownup, as the grownups were busy catching up other grownups, or busy rocking in silence, sucking their teeth and hmming now and then to the tick of the mantel clock. In that era, the forties and fifties, and in that country-heartland-frontier culture, grandparents claimed little of their grandchildren. They seemed to settle for watching their grandkids from afar.

In my early teens, a deeper connection developed, when my younger brother and I spent a week with Grandmother and Granddaddy, for three summers. I discovered that they did a lot more work on non-Sundays. They were busy before we woke up and stayed busy, right up to dinner. But they did their work without reference to us and left Dick and me to play or relax or read on our own. Sometimes they let us slop the hogs, gather eggs, feed the chickens, or pull hay from the mow to feed horses. But we were mostly unaware of how they spent their time. At meals and reading under the light and smell of kerosene lamps after dinner, we developed somewhat deeper bonds, but they seemed temporary, largely dissolving when our visit was over with.

The *Diary of Mrs. C. E. Childers* covers thirty-two and a half months of the Great Depression era, from April 16, 1932 through December 31, 1934, in 36 pages. That's the extent of it. It's likely that this was Grandmother's only diary, for she didn't throw things away, and her possessions were thoroughly sifted by Aunt Evelyn after Grandmother died.

Grandmother and Granddaddy started their family late and kept it small: my father, William Allen, who was 14 when the diary begins, and his sister, Evelyn Daisy, who was 18. Grandmother was 47.

I have no idea what motivated her to keep a diary. By her own record, those weren't momentous years in her life. Surely, she didn't have to document her activities to certify that she was fully occupied; observing her would be certification enough. Nor was she codifying her activities, for there's nary an instruction, recipe, or prescription in those pages; or making a guidebook for coming seasons (when to prune the apple tree, when to clean the coal cellar), as she had been performing such chores supposedly on schedule for 20 years of housekeeping. And she most certainly didn't use those ruled pages to reflect, ventilate, inhale, exhale, or the like, for there's not an internal, personal word in the 990 days. Perhaps the diary was intended to convey to her daughter, Aunt Evelyn, what life would be like as a farm wife and mother. I don't know.

Grandmother was no Virginia Woolf. Daisy Margaret Childers doesn't record reactions, passions, convictions, rants, lyric idylls. She doesn't diarize life's conundrums or inner conflicts—or outer conflicts, for that matter. She keeps a simple ledger of key words, a daybook of activity in the simplest terms: the date followed by sentences than which there can be none shorter: a verb with the subject understood: "[I] sewed," "[it] rained, [I] washed." Sometimes she augments the verb with a subject, object, or adverb, like "sprouted potatoes," or "tied tob. [tobacco]," "Franks here" (meaning Frank and his family visited), "bank robbed." On rare occasions the prose turns relatively florid with a prepositional phrase, as in "canned tomatoes for Lewis," "snowed made dress for Babe," but that's about as expansive as it gets. The closest she gets to feelings is exclaiming over a February day with the word "beautiful"—the only evaluative word in 990 days. Stingy with words, stingy with punctuation, stingy with emotion.

Nor is it the kind of diary that needed a lock, for there are no bodies buried there.

Here's an excerpt from the beginning of the diary:

[1932, May]

19 went to Ina's to wash Graduation
  that nite. Hale Miller's baby was born.
20 set out tomatoe plants
21 went to town [with] Charles, boy, and Babe
  [Granddaddy, my father, Aunt Evelyn]
22 went to Sunday School and preaching
23 plowed potatoes took up carpet
  went to revival meeting that nite

In the beginning of the diary, she starts each day on a separate line (five days on seven lines, above), and the length of the entries mostly warrants it. But by October her entries become shorter and, perhaps out of parsimony, begin running together. By November, a section of the diary looks like this, 14 days on seven lines:

2 Ironed 3 cleaned cellar 4 at Lewis
5 cleaned smoke house. 6 went to church revival started.
7 washed 8 election. Ironed churned.
  Frank came home with boy.
9 & 10. Housework 11 at Lewis 12 Sat work
13 S.S. Revival at nite 14 washed 15 ironed

I began wondering if word count might show something, so I counted and clustered her words. Grandmother's tersity and consistent and frequent use of words made it easy. Over 990 days, I counted 1157 nouns or noun phrases—mentions of things.

Household Work. The prize for mentioned things goes to recurring household chores. Washing, ironing, sewing/mending, and cleaning the house and various outbuildings and cellars account for about 40 percent of all items in the diary. That includes the mysterious "Saturday's work" (which no living relative has been able to define) and infrequent household chores, like painting, stretching fence, sawing wood, taking up rugs, and setting up the Franklin stove.

Work Outside the House. The garden or field draws focus on many additional days—about 10 percent of all mentions—to planting, making beds, and plowing (once); and, at the other end of the cycle, harvesting fruits and vegetables and tying tobacco for drying. A smaller set of work routines—another 8 percent—comprise canning activities (often outside the house) from late spring into autumn and butchering various animals when their time has come.

Work Without End. Mentions of some sort of labor for Daisy are many compared to other kinds of mentions (58% or so); but they seem too few for life on a subsistence farm. My visits with Grandmother and Granddaddy and conversations with relatives decades ago altered that picture dramatically. The diary disregards the many routines of the day-to-day: putting three meals on the table without benefit of electricity, plumbing, or cooking fuel; keeping a flock of chickens; gathering eggs; tending hatchling chicks, slopping hogs, and so on. And simple words like "washed" or "ironed" don't convey that washing entailed building a fire in the kitchen stove to heat water, hauling in water from the pump for washing and then again for rinsing, scrubbing on a laundry board with lye soap that she made herself, putting the wet goods through a hand-cranked wringer, and hanging things to dry in the side yard; and that ironing, while more straight forward, required another fire on another day so she could wield a hot flat iron.

Bound up in many of the work mentions is a thread of communal farm life, a vestige of frontier culture, where you can't get along without the help of others: cooking, canning, washing, ironing, gardening, and harvesting *for others,* or *at other's houses,* gathering to re-roof a neighbor's barn, butchering sheep at a friend's or relative's, and cleaning the church yard. I'm sure these activities carried with them feel-good moments of community and happy interplay. But they were still work.

As it spills out of the diary directly and implied, Grandmother's work life looks oppressive. On top of that, life's passages contribute to the weight of her days: only one birth and a couple of commencements. But death, burial, and funerals crop up on virtually every page.

[1933 January]

6 finished tying tob[acco] *7 cleaned house Buried Ella Warren sold cows 8 Mr Henry Woods buried 9 Sore throat* [continuing through 17] ... *27 rained. Cofers Baby buried.*

What must have been most sad—although sadness wasn't recorded—ran:

[1932 July]

On the 28th *"canned corn for Flossie...."* On the 29th *"washed for myself";* on the 30th *"Took her* [Flossie] *to the hospital."* The days of July 31 through August 5 are blank and on the 6th: *"Died,* [I] *came home from hospital."*

Flossie was Daisy's youngest sister.

Over the notations of work and assorted tragedies, a number of social events—albeit, a little less than a quarter of the entries—sprinkle intimations of life enjoyed, even though joy or anything close to it is never explicit. The major diversion was visiting: sitting with others and talking. This shows in the many visits back and forth with friends, neighbors, Daisy's large extended family—especially her nearby brother, my Great Uncle Lewis. Things that could be construed as real fun could be counted on less than a full set of fingers and toes: bean dinners in town; ice cream suppers at the church; a high school play; baccalaureate ceremonies (if I am truly generous to an event that in my experience has been almost invariably tedious); and a couple of references to a "party."

From my first years, I probably always knew that Grandmother and Granddaddy were poor. But I was still oblivious to their hard-scrabble existence. Now, in the terse light of Grandmother's entries, unsoftened by evaluative adjectives and adverbs, I conjured up a grubbing, mirthless, and stoic existence.

Even with the social events and the instances of recorded fun, the upshot of Daisy Childers' diary is as grey as the background of the photocopied pages and humorless—pages of recurring tasks and events related to subsisting and its inverse, dying. And it wasn't just the Great Depression making its mark on their well-being. Long after the good times had returned, after the end of World War II, when I knew them first-hand, there was nothing about the farm or their lives that could contradict the diary, that led me to believe that they were worse off in the diary years than in the years of national prosperity.

The bleakness that seeps out of her journal can also be laid to Grandmother's brevity and the absence of words of emotion. Entries are void of self, inner processes, reactions—at times of great sad moment, like Flossie's death, or lesser sad moment, like when the red pup ran away; or at times of happy moment, like when a sister comes to visit, or a party. Should I chalk up the deficit of words and especially words of feeling to Daisy's stoic approach to life? Or to verbal parsimony? Or to precious little time for the daily jot? Or, if I allow myself to strip the family bare, to the Childers's genetic inclination to being underwhelmed by emotions and, when they do well up, of expressing them guardedly if at all?

So I call on my time with the flesh-and-blood grandparents for a more complete picture, when I knew them beyond the pages of the diary and knew that she and Granddaddy experienced joy: engaged happily with a large, close circle of relatives and friends, went off to church with a purpose, reveled in helping others, and—who knows?—drew steady satisfaction from those seemingly endless chores.

And I call on my time without them, the time after high school, when I left them behind and began evolving into an easternized, citified, opera-going, aetheistic, liberal, member of the upper middle class—a being unrecognizable to them, or alien, or intolerable—

and measure the shocking huge gulf between them as were and me as is—and admit that whatever particle of them or the farm was in me had slipped away. What I have left of Grandmother is the image of her ever-toiling, productive persona—augmented by her real self's calm affection and warm feed-sack-clothed bulk—and a tiny photograph of her on the mantel in my study, bonneted as she always was outdoors, feeding the chickens on what might have been a one-word-diary-entry day.

INCREMENTS OF SELF

9

My Father's Violin

Musical misadventures, despite a musical father.

Whatever was being taught or whoever was teaching it, I don't remember. I know that I was eight and in my third-grade classroom at Western Elementary School, and that at some point a beautiful black-haired woman walked in. She introduced herself as Miss Thompson, the school's music teacher, and asked if anyone would be interested in taking violin lessons. It was free, she said, and all you needed was a violin.

My father had a violin. I was certain that Dad's violin wasn't my violin and that I needed some time to think over the idea of lessons. So I didn't respond. But mouthy Billy Fisher, who lived on our block, volunteered, "Tommy has a violin." He must have been walking by our house one day when the windows were open and heard Dad playing.

Miss Thompson ushered me to the hall, where I revealed that the violin in question was not mine, but my father's. Notwithstanding, she recruited me on the spot to begin lessons if I got permission from the violin's owner.

My Dad treasured two possessions: one was his collection of carpentry tools; the other was his violin. The tools lay shiny and lightly oiled in a shellacked oak toolbox with chrome fittings; it was off limits to children. The violin and its bow lived in a black leatherette case lined with faded purple velvet. It, too, was off-limits. But I had seen it many times, when Dad took it out to play. The violin's shell and scroll were burnished the color of a chestnut horse's flank, the pegs and fingerboard were stained black, the bow was horsehair on an ebony-colored stick.

When I brought home Miss Thompson's proposal, my parents became excited, in the bridled, suppressed Childers kind of way. It seemed natural that I take up music, and the violin seemed almost preternatural, for Dad was a violinist and I was my father's son and so on. They smiled and murmured, and Dad said, "Yes, you may use the violin."

Permission. No pressure. Well, except the pressure of expectation—not theirs, mine—my expectation that my musician father would necessarily have begat a first-born musical enough to secure the musical legacy.

With their pleasure, my uncertainty turned to a moderate excitement. "OK. Thanks," I said. Immediately, weekly lessons began at school and daily practice began at home.

To spare my family the screeching of an abused violin and me the embarrassment of bringing so much pain to the instrument and to my family, I practiced upstairs in my brother's and my bedroom or in the basement. But noble consideration wasn't enough: the house was so small that the noise couldn't be damped. The strings yowled like multiple cats being stretched, one for each string. Our dog, who had always been drawn to cats in a predatory way, would sit beside the music stand and bay like a coyote as I practiced.

So the practice went, day after day and year after year. The caterwauling of a tormented violin turned into a primary sound that I carried forward from my childhood.

Two years later, in the fifth grade, violin lessons and practice persisted, but the breakthrough that the family was praying would bestow some fluency on my playing didn't occur. My parents, perhaps stared down by the handwriting on the wall, decided to diversify. They scraped together $25 and bought a used upright piano. Again, it seemed that, since my father was a master of this instrument as well, maybe the piano and I were congenitally destined for each other. I was also motivated knowing that Mom—who wasn't a bit musical—liked the idea of being entertained by tickled ivories while she cooked or ironed, and of showing off a talented son to her lady friends.

And the image—make that mirage—of making music that I enjoyed listening to (classical and light classical) and perhaps the hope of fulfilling Mom's small dream led me willingly into the piano caper and laid upon me another musical self-expectation.

Continuing with the violin, I began piano lessons with Mrs. Kane, a few houses away. She was a wide woman with, I thought, fingers too stubby to play the piano. But she did, and very well. From the outset of practicing, it was clear that the piano, whose strings are simply hammered, offered a smaller margin of error than the violin, whose strings require accuracy of fingering, apt pressure of the fingers, vibration of the finger, and bowing of varied strength, all at the same time; and that the piano would wrack my family's nerves less than the violin. It seemed to me that with fewer technical minutiae to master, I would hit pay dirt sooner with the piano.

Violin continued, during the school year, with the directive to practice during the summer months. Piano persisted twelve months of the year.

In addition to violin and piano, I signed up for the school chorus on the opening day of the seventh grade, shouldering one more musical self-expectation. Again, it seemed logical, even bio-logical, as Dad was an accomplished baritone. He had sung in his middle teens with his mother at funerals and weddings and was currently a stalwart in the Methodist choir in town.

Later in that first week of seventh grade, I met with Miss Thompson in the music room. It was the start of violin year five. She asked me to play a simplified phrase from Brahms' Lullaby, from the year before. But in the doldrums of summer vacation, my practicing had foundered, and I could barely eke out a solid note. She stopped me and suggested one of the early practice pieces from the first year, five years earlier: "Twinkle Twinkle Little Star." Even for a boy whose expectations of self, musical or otherwise, weren't all that high, this was too degrading.

I packed the instrument in its case and walked it home to my father, for all time. Mom was clearly disappointed. I think Dad had seen (heard) it coming; he didn't seem upset. Nonetheless, the violin expectations of Mom, Dad, and me lay in splinters before us. Never mind that we would nevermore be threatened by my torturous abuse of that instrument.

Piano went on. Under Mrs. Kane I eventually mastered a simple transcription of the waltz from Gounod's *Faust* and even played it in a recital at the Methodist Church. But as with the violin, so too the piano. My attention waned. Mom's gentle reminders to practice weren't enough to get me to plant myself in front of the upright for more than a half hour or so between lessons—and eventually not even that—no matter how much time I had on my hands.

Whether for that reason or some other, Mrs. Kane turned me over to a talented high-school senior, the Collins girl, who lived at the end of the block, to whom I thereafter handed my 25 cents each week. By this time I was likely to forget to practice from one week to the next and, after a few months of sessions that regressed my skills, embarrassed me, and pissed off the lovely Miss Collins, she sent me and my weekly quarter packing. I went home to my end of the block and confessed to Mom and Dad that I had been expelled from piano. Neither was surprised.

A sop to my musical heritage, my singing seemed to prosper. Not only was my voice buried behind the singing of twenty other children, the director coddled us with straightforward vocal pablum like "The Lost Chord," "I Dream of Jeannie," "Oh Danny Boy," and the ilk. The chorus and I honeymooned for two years, until the director learned of a choral competition and assigned us more challenging works. Which meant more complex harmonies, which in turn meant singing one note when your neighbor was singing another. Suddenly, my steadfast tone began wandering from my own to my neighbor's note. Sticking to my part proved dicey. Moreover, my voice was starting to growl and quaver at unexpected moments; it was changing.

I didn't re-up for chorus the next fall, and I didn't mention it to my parents.

Mom was eager to see me succeed in music and if it could draw a bit of attention to my recessive personage, all the better. As I was girding my social loins for entry into high school, Mom was plotting my musical future and lit on the tuba. It was a brilliant choice. Not only didn't it require a sunk cost, being one of the few instruments that the school provided, it was a virtual shoo-in to the high school marching band, which is where my mother wanted to see me: in uniform and marching proud.

I liked the instrument enough. It was big and showy, and it had only three keys. How hard could that be? And the tuba placed me automatically and immediately in Junior Orchestra, which had been the feeder for the marching band, time out of mind.

So when classes began in the ninth grade, I started tuba lessons with Mr. DeWitt Thorton, the leader of all of Chillicothe High School's musical enterprises, and found my seat in the Junior Orchestra.

One day, toward the end of the first semester, the stalwarts of Junior Orchestra were sawing and blowing and banging the bejesus out of some simple piece, possibly a Sibelius. In the middle of a bar, Mr. Thornton drew his baton sharply down, directing us to stop. We dribbled to a halt. With frozen face, in basso profundo, he stated that, in two months of practice, this edition of Junior Orchestra had not improved, that we were getting worse rather than better, and that it was the result of apathy and lack of practice. He sounded almost tearful, but in the tuba section I was too far away to see tears. He concluded that, notwithstanding the long history and traditions of Chillicothe High, he was compelled to disband Junior Orchestra.

With that judgment, which any court in the land would have upheld, Mr. Thornton nipped in the bud my mother's hope for a band-strutting son, and for all time quashed my family's passion for finding the musician in me. Mom and Dad now had no doubt that if they were ever to point to me with pride, it would not be for my musicianship.

The tuba went back to the school. The piano found another home, for $35. In time, my voice smoothed out, but it would be use-able only in the shower and now and then at party sing-alongs after sufficient wine.

One by one my self-imposed musical expectations had come up short. But I couldn't quite shake the conviction that I should be able to play an instrument and that there was an instrument out there simple enough to be mastered without much effort. In a last-ditch effort, I took up the recorder, but practice began puny and died early, and the beautiful pear-wood recorder brought final closure to my music making.

A few years later, I learned that my brother, who never put hand or lip to an instrument, decided in his thirties to give the guitar a whirl. If he'd taken me as a fraternal predictor of success, he could have saved the time and money; his effort fared no better than any of mine. Somehow that made me feel better—not because he had failed as I had, but because it pointed to a congenital link between us; by both of us embodying the a-musicality of our mother's line, we somehow had a stronger brotherhood.

Dad died many years later. His violin, that tannic beauty, found its way to me, since I was the only survivor who had had any connection to it. As I write this, it's leaning into a corner of my study—an ironic, corrupted, disconsolate piece of wood, an instru-ment of unrequited hope—in its purple-velvet-lined black-leather-ette coffin.

10

Small Man on Campus

Fending for food and identity in a megaversity.

When I first set foot on campus I felt like a tadpole in a large murky pond. The vast acreage of Parking Lot C, alone, shrank me and my little green VW bug to insignificance.

In 1958, the College Park campus of the University of Maryland boasted about 40,000 students scattered across a dizzying range of disciplines. It didn't help that I declared my major in one of the largest, English literature, which counted its devotees in the thousands. My social life was nil, as I was plugged into nothing social on campus or off. I lived at home, with Mom, Dad, and brother Dick, about a mile from campus. When I wasn't studying, I was doing ordinary things with the family— meals, of course, and household chores, and some interactions with friends of the family. I also spent a lot of time taking in the culture and vibes of the big city, Washington, DC, sometimes with my brother, sometimes on my own, sometimes with the whole family.

But fresh from a town in Ohio where small was the rule (house, streets, overall scale) and faced with a gigantic metropolis and a megaversity, I knew immediately that I would have to fabricate a niche where I could secure my own identity. My first step was to take a clerical job at the university library the summer before I matriculated. That helped, providing some social interaction during the hours at work, and even a few hours of after-work dalliance with co-workers. The library job continued, part time, for my whole four years.

I took up Latin as my minor, under the pretense of having a rare specialization should I end up as a high-school teacher, but really, I knew even then, to winnow down my anonymity. The courses barely drew 4 or 5 students, and the University sported a mere two classicists, who covered both Greek and Latin. Small classes, small faculty, small pond-within-a-big-pond.

Sometime in my sophomore year I took a non-credit silk-screening course with a guy who made silk-screen posters, fliers, and the like for campus groups, in a small workroom in the Student Union. When he graduated, he offered the job to me. I coughed up something like $25 for the equipment and took over, even though we both knew that I wasn't nearly as talented as he: one network channel was already devoting 5 minutes of early-evening news to his clever lip-synching puppets. Rather, muppets. He was Jim Henson.

In the summer before my junior year, my father was transferred to California, so I rented a bed in a student boarding house in College Park. Life proceeded without incident that year.

The next year I rented lodging in a rooming house off campus, sharing a bedroom-study-bath with another student, Barry, also a senior. I continued as a study nerd, but my outgoing roommate— an extroverted and varied and engaged kind of guy—shoved me a few crumbs off his active social plate, such as a part in a small play with the French club, and planning the French club picnic.

On the lookout for cheap food, I took on a third job, as a busboy for a sorority. The sorority was—probably still is—housed in a semi-circle of 13 identical coral-colored brick-colonial, three-story mansions at the foot of the campus, on the south side of Route 1. "My" sorority was about medium-high on the pecking order of sororities. Its name may have been Sigma Delta, but I'm not sure. Tri-

Delt was number one, boasting the prettiest, most talented, richest, and most self-congratulatory girls on campus. The girls of Sigma Delta, if that's the name, were unaffected and fun.

Busing—job number three—provided all my lunches and dinners, except Saturday evening through Sunday, indenturing me for about an hour at each service. The kitchen and dining room were in the basement. The girls fended for themselves at breakfast, walking into the kitchen whenever they stumbled out of bed, to get a plate or bowl of whatever Cook had prepared. Busboy presence was not required, but for some reason I was in the kitchen at breakfast time once and saw the parade of girls—some in bathrobes, some dressed for class, and all in hair-curlers. For lunch and dinner, we four busboys moved the food from kitchen to table; fetched water, ketchup, more of this, more of that; cleared the tables; and washed the dishes. We ate before the girls came down.

Cook's name was Annie. She was a round, middle-aged, friendly African-American woman with a southern accent—perhaps just Maryland-style southern. She called me "Tome." She treated us boys well, and always gave us enough to eat. Her cuisine was ordinaire. She made a bland but edible lasagna, pretty good baked chicken, ordinary puddings for dessert. She rarely created disasters. You didn't take that kind of job for fine food. You took it for free eats. If you found a few good times on the side socializing with the other busboys and the girls, and found the food more palatable than you thought your dorm-bound contemporaries were getting, so much the better.

Supporting my English major and Latin minor in my senior year didn't demand a lot of attention. So I pledged a social fraternity, Alpha Tau Omega, to breathe life into my arid social life and, significantly, to further enhance my sense of being other than a flea on the university behemoth. ATO was one of the two dominant frats on campus. I repressed the fact that it was founded on conservative-Christian, anti-Semitic, racist principles. But what did I care at the time? They wanted this "older" guy for my grades, to keep the academicians off their back, and I wanted them for the fun. In my pledge term, I brought them a 4-point average and they introduced me to alcohol. The former made me feel good about myself; the latter made me feel ... good.

After the final exams of the next term, this flea graduated from the UM behemoth, in good grade-point, emotional, and social standing. I bade farewell to the Latin minor clique, the rooming house and roommate, the library job, the poster business, the sorority food service, and the late-stage fraternity gambit—the niches of my survival.

11

Out and About

Stepping out of a long-term closet, good sense to the contrary.

It was late spring in 1968. I woke up to crows coughing outside my window and an inkling, like the ghost of a finger at my back, propelling me toward something.

After a couple of years in the Army, and serving out the years I owed Baltimore County Public Library for financing my master's degree, I had taken the gutsy tack of pursuing a PhD in library and information science, in order to fast-track my career into directing a large library or to secure a faculty or research position. By a happy coincidence, Congress, in order to recruit more people to pursue the PhD in the field, had just passed a bill of generous funding. I also drew on the GI Bill.

At the end of the first year in the Ph.D. program, at Rutgers, New Brunswick, I believed that I could actually walk away with the degree. My grades had fared better than I had dared imagine and I aced the two weeks of written prelims. All I had left was the thesis research and its defense.

School had recessed for the summer. My few buddies in New Brunswick had fled the hallowed halls for hometowns, vacations, or summer jobs. I was alone and feeling it. I had no job to occupy me, no vacation spot tugging at me, and only a semblance of a hometown—my parents' place outside Denver, where they had lived for just a couple of years. I would simply stay put in New Brunswick and work up a thesis topic.

Mid-afternoon of that first day I was at my desk in my apartment. The desk was a flea-market Victorian dressing table with a full-length mirror between two pedestals across which I'd bolted a full sheet of 3/8-inch marine-grade plywood. As I sat there, face to face with me, trying to think of research possibilities, my thoughts began to turn inward, that ghost of a finger once again touching the middle of my back. Out of the muck of my mind a hulk rose up, pushed that digit hard into my spine, and rumbled, "Gay or straight, man; what'll it be?"

Although surprised to be questioning myself, I was not caught completely off guard. I had had a few isolated passive-sex encounters of the gay kind over the years and had chosen to dismiss them as the unexceptional excesses that are allowed any young person.

I had dated during high school, college, the master's studies and the Army. Most of the dates were uneventful and didn't stick to my brain. I remember one in high school where my date, also a member of the Latin Club, was so terrified that I was going to do something untoward that she rode on the farthest possible side of the passenger seat, pressed like a coat of paint against her door. When I opened it to escort her back to her anxious parents, she pretty near fell out.

I don't remember whom I took to the Junior Prom; and I sat out the Senior Prom with a couple of other guys who thought proms were "silly."

From college I remember a couple of dates—pleasant, if not hot: a perky fox-faced coed from the sorority house where I bused tables; a stunning black-haired beauty from another sorority whom I took to several of my fraternity's parties (I think she was enamored of my big fraternity's cachet, rather than mine); an antic and squirrely girl who wanted me to visit her dorm room at night; a pretty blond who told me on our second date that she had, after all, decided to accept her erstwhile boyfriend's proposal of marriage.

Once I was working, in the Baltimore area, I dated a myopic young woman with the only truly opalescent skin I have ever seen who also informed me on the second date that she had decided to accept a pending proposal of marriage. And another, who pursued me for three years almost against my will, all but to the point of betrothal.

I remember most the one in the Army, whom I dated regularly for over a year: Charlotte, a pretty browned-haired sweetie who was embarked on a radio career. She was the one I was most ardent about; but I never said the L word or asked the subsequent question. I left the Army and never saw her again.

Now I was 28, no longer a youth, asking myself the question that in its very asking implied that those dismissed gay encounters just might be defining ones.

I had always been given to Venn diagrams, matrices, and mathematical logic. So I took out a sheet of paper, drew a line down the middle, and started writing: on the left, the likely negative consequences of being gay; on the right, the likely positives. Not that this balance sheet represented anything approaching authority, for I knew, and only remotely, exactly one person who was to my knowledge gay, and I had read—in a subplot that could suitably have been labeled Avoidance—nothing on the subject.

For a long while I scanned my mind for things to add, things to delete, or clarifications, all the while looking for a reason to send the beast back to the muck and bury the primordial question.

The listing came to an end. My face in the mirror was grey, like the beast. The cons on the list far outnumbered the pros, and the message of the list was clear: the straight path would lead to a life of open relationships, unfettered pursuit of professional goals, easy travel in the mainstream of workplace and society; the gay path would lead to a life constrained by the dominant fear and loathing of gays at the time, to a social and professional swamp of subterfuge, paths not taken, and selves not realized—such as seeking only gay-friendly work environments, or avoiding the exposure of public prominence, or dissimulating endlessly about my sexual being. Gay life would be far less than a bowl of cherries.

But the discussion with myself wasn't about logic and ratiocination. It was about taking the blinders off. The ritual of reasoning uncovered my core. I wadded up the list, my life's balance sheet, banked it off the mirror and into the wastebasket for two points, and took the next Greyhound bus into The City of All Possibilities. At the New York City Port Authority Bus Terminal an inner GPS (male voice, eager, panting) took over and led me to the West Village and into my first gay bar.

12

Where I Ought to Be

Called, without sarcasm,
to a career of some meaning and good.

On first hearing, the tune was so captivating that the words didn't register. On second hearing, the lyrics took: "'Tis the gift to be simple, 'tis the gift to be free, 'Tis the gift to come down where we ought to be ...." Words from celibate utopians of the early 20th century, the Shakers, words that teased me with the possibility of finding a place, maybe even in this life, where one—I—*ought* to be. Never mind that abstinence from sexual congress led the Shakers to the door of extinction, their words rang for me.

Beginning in high school, I thought about where I ought to be in terms of a career and talked with my parents about it. They never used the word "ought." Pretty much the opposite. Dad made it clear that I could find satisfaction just about anywhere I landed. He quietly insisted that hard work and honesty would reward me with satisfaction. I'm not sure why I believed this, as Dad had busted a nut escaping life on a farm, but I did. Another word my parents didn't use in discussing vocations was "calling." It implies "ought," but it smacked too much of divine intervention and fundamentalist Christianity for their taste. Mom and Dad simply hoped that I could find a career that satisfied me and where I could do some good. They had been teachers, and that kind of career-coupled-with-good—as opposed to hoodwinking simple folk into buying insurance they didn't need or peddling used cars—seemed natural for me, and I subscribed heartily to the idea.

Beginning in junior high, a career direction began to form, unbeknownst to me.

There was nothing unusual in a kid visiting the local Carnegie library as I regularly did in junior high and high school, drawn first to Baum's Oz novels and travel-adventure tales, then to the classics of English, American, and French literature. But for this kid, those visits turned out to predestine where I ought to be.

One day, in the car with my father when I was perhaps 15 or 16, midway between the Dairy Queen and the High Street Pharmacy, he suggested that I might want to consider a library career. I don't know where he came up with that idea, but I felt a glimmer of direction. In the coming years it seemed to be serially confirmed, as I was drawn to a part-time job in my university library that I kept until I graduated, to a summer as a pre-professional librarian on a bookmobile covering the far reaches of Prince Georges County, Maryland, through a year of the Library Science degree at Rutgers, and on into my first professional post as a reference and young-adult librarian for Baltimore County.

When I was drafted into the Army—immediately after starting that job with Baltimore County, in the fall of '62—I was faced with two years of career path interruptus. But Destiny continued its pull. Before I even had a permanent assignment at Fort Lewis, it propelled me across the street from my temporary barracks into the craft shop and a transcendent encounter with a woman puttering over a mosaic coffee table. She happened to be the Post Librarian. Had I not met her, I would surely have spent my days as a company clerk. Instead, I was assigned to the Fort Lewis public libraries (for that is what post libraries are) and became, once again, a public librarian—now in fatigues—running the North Fort Branch for my two years of Armed servitude.

The career pathway detoured for a few months while I considered diverting to architecture, but it got on its regular route again after my discharge and led me, now in civvies, back to libraryland.

Years later I learned that people are propelled into a library career—or used to be, before the severely etherized state of today's information world—through one of three passions, the first being the romance of the printed page and its lore, data, disquisitions, and depictions expanding outward, infinitely.

Second, the thirst for library research, sleuthing down the real story, the definitive "truth" of a topic or question.

Third, the order that libraries impose on random-seeming heaps of recorded things.

It was the latter that propelled me—the intellectual systems that organize those heaps into logical arrays and overlay them with finding tools. For me, the draw was less about being up close and intimate with the library's stock in trade and more about mechanisms that make libraries work.

After I had plied the public library trade for a couple of years, and before the excitement of the reference desk dissolved into tedium, my oughta-pilot fired up again and drove me into a PhD program in library and information science. I wasn't at all sure that I had the requisite brain power and endurance for a research degree, but destiny would not be denied. Braced for washing out, I cashed in more sweat equity than I knew I had and completed the course work honorably and the qualifying exam with praise from the profs. The thesis work, where most PhD aspirants wipe out, was—can you say this without being a theist?—blessed. Terry Crowley, two years ahead of me in the program, had begun to gnaw over how accurately librarians answered simple questions of fact—a standard role of public and academic libraries. For his thesis, he sent proxy users into New Jersey libraries, like comparison shoppers, to pose questions and record the responses. Then he judged the quality of the responses.

I went a step further and studied whether New Jersey's stronger libraries (richer, better-staffed, etc.) answered questions accurately more often than weaker libraries—questions like *Who is the poet laureate of the United States? What was the federal budget expenditure in 1936? Who painted the "Yellow Christ"? What is the gap specification for the 1963 Chevy Corvair? What does the OJ in OJ Simpson stand for? What is this piece of poetry from: "O pardon me, thou bleeding piece of earth..."?*

Crowley and I both found that the correctness of answers was far less than the close-to-100%-perfect that libraryland assumed. Back at research headquarters (my tiny carrel in the library) there was sometimes horror at the responses, as when one respondent protested that libraries don't answer questions like that, or sometimes ha-ha's, as when another respondent answered that "O pardon me, thou bleeding piece of earth ...." came from Shakespeare's play "Ibid."

When our findings were released—particularly my more scientifically based results pointing to a 55-65 percent correctness rate—the public library world went into shock, and two stars were born, Terry and me. Even before I had received the degree (June 1970), I was published in refereed and popular library journals and being called to consult. So finding a job was a cinch. Dumb luck or intuition kicked in on the job hunt, diverting me from the academic slough of the Illinois library school and the cutting edge of the Syracuse University library school in a bleak Syracuse setting, to the promise of the Drexel's school being remade and the rich metropolis of Philadelphia.

A new assistant prof has to deliver courses right off the bat. If she's totally unwashed and has no academic courses in her knapsack, she will either get lucky and take over courses that someone else has already scripted or, unlucky, must invent courses from scratch. The courses assigned to me were all scratch. They were either new to the curriculum or the previous instructors had scarpered, leaving no trail of content.

In the first year, I built courses on too flimsy an intellectual foundation (too hurried, too lazy, too distracted by other duties), and a couple of them turned out dismal. Add to that the common impostor syndrome that's rampant among academics—the shrinking dread that at any moment you will be stripped naked in your own field of expertise, half-wrong, all wrong, faking data, faking conclusions, a charlatan and a fraud—and those new courses made me squirm. As the curriculum evolved, they were relegated to the waste basket, with my blessing.

A couple of other courses became respectable with reiteration. And two made me feel I belonged in the classroom, especially Management of Library and Information Services, which stood the test of external reviews from management faculty and endured for thirty years.

The thesis accompanied me to Drexel, of course, and I used it as a base to continue testing issues of service quality—as a springboard to more research and publication, research funding, consulting and, in an admittedly small pond, a national and international reputation. The thesis and its follow-ons also found their way into some of my courses.

Gradually I tapped whatever natural management talent I had and added administrative roles to my repertoire: informal team leader, formal team leader, then interim dean and finally, as I left the classroom behind, associate dean.

Drexel was rich soil. The students of the college—all graduate students in my courses—were not just willing, but eager to work hard and learn. The college administration welcomed innovation, and the university administration at least tolerated it. I had the time to do research and write. And the administrative duties were largely gratifying. It was a good place to land.

I had progressed, stepwise, to the eye of a career and to the I of purpose. A found, stumbled-upon, seemingly accidental purpose, but a true one. A centerpiece whose center was not me, but the goodness that it produced—in this case, outfitting the next generation of people to manage, safeguard, and share the record of human knowledge. Mom and Dad, convinced that I had arrived at a career that I reveled in and that by its nature contributed to the greater good, were overjoyed. Ordinarily inordinately modest about themselves, they were to the end of their days blatantly proud of their two sons, the doctor of medicine making people better in Florida and the doctor of philosophy, me, sowing my good here and abroad.

I had come down where I ought to be. Called, as it were.

13

Tropics of Comfort

*Finding zones of peace and contentment
in the wild and wooly gay Mecca of Provincetown.*

I didn't come out to myself till 1968. I had probably been building my proverbial closet starting ten years before, in college, when the social norm of a hetero life was starting to feel like a suit made for someone else. Eventually the closet was stifling—overflowing with all the wrong outfits—such as dates with women and close encounters with hetero betrothals—and swarming with my own masquerades. At the age of 28, I opened the door.

... to an immediate blast of liberation. But that faded in the face of an undercurrent of worries—zones of discomfort—that I had only vaguely imagined before turning that fateful doorknob: first, declaring myself—to myself—as gay; second, navigating my way through, finding a place in, the gay milieu; and third, coming to grips with the global loathing of gay people by the rest of society.

Simply counting myself as a member of a denigrated population should be enough to trigger the lowest of low-self-esteem, as it did for countless others who heeded their inner call to gayness. Surprisingly, there was little of this in me. Perhaps I had processed it subconsciously for a long time and grown used to the idea. But also, I'm certain that I owe some of my relative comfort in this area to two short exchanges with my father.

When I was 10 or so, about 1950, Dad and I were standing on a street corner in Chillicothe waiting for a traffic light to change. I mentioned how some of the kids in school liked to joke around and call other kids "queer." Dad said that was not an OK thing to call other people. I knew that the word meant approximately something about unnatural gender attraction, and I learned once again that Dad was against devaluing others.

Another time, when I was in my teens, he revealed, gesturing to his groinal area, that Danny, husband to Dad's cousin Eulah, had offered Dad fellatio. I don't remember his words, but I knew that he had declined. I also knew from his words and tone that Dad wasn't being pejorative, just calmly descriptive of the incident, although puzzled by Danny's ability to keep Eulah happy sexually: "Well, he did give her two daughters," Dad allowed.

So, when I finally came out, I was pretty much at ease listing my name on the gay side of life's ledger. But unease on two other dimensions remained: knowing and accommodating to the gay subculture; and facing the universal rejection of me and my kind by the straight world.

The first of these—my fit into my new world—was the only one I could conceive of addressing.

Not long before I declared myself gay, I could have been counted among the masses who mocked homosexuals. Actually, I didn't mock, thanks to my father's teachings, but sat silently and hypocritically off to the side as others held forth. Stereotypes were the best targets of derision—men light of gait, limp of wrist, lispish of speech, femme in appearance, and so on. The general public believed the stereotypes. Even the American Psychiatric Association classified homosexuality as a psychiatric disorder back then. New research that would uncover homosexual origins, behaviors, milieus, population statistics, and sexual practices existed, but had yet to reach the popular media. I could have sought out those early tweedy writings, but decided instead, to take the plunge in real time, blind to the gay realities.

Even then—a year before the Stonewall riots—it seemed common knowledge that Fire Island, a 30-mile-long sand spit off the southern shore of Long Island, was a gay watering hole. So I packed myself and a bag of clothes into my old dark-green convertible, TR-4 with a knife slash in the roof and drove out to Long Island. I picked a town on the south side (Bayshore, was it?), and followed the signs to the ferry. As soon as we cast off, I noticed that the boat's demographic was 99 ½ percent male-female couples with children, and ½ percent me. When we docked, the figures got worse. No lone males except me, and no paired males. It was clearly the wrong part of Fire Island. I took the return ferry, and that was that.

Back at Rutgers, I settled into working up a thesis proposal. But on the peripheries of my work, I was on high alert for clues to gay gathering places. Without any literature to guide me, and not even knowing if any existed, I *gleaned*. The *New York Times* reviewed certain books that skirted gay life; newspapers reported on homosexual run-ins with the law; and some mainstream authors, such as Gore Vidal and James Baldwin, dealt directly, if fictionally, with gay life. From simple word count, my gleanings pointed to an age-old artist colony on Cape Cod. The next Labor Day weekend, in that same old TR-4, I blew into Provincetown.

P-town captured me as it had captured generations—September days filled with sun and a trace of humidity that lay on bare skin like thin flannel; the charm of a very old wood-framed, white-steepled New England village; and the walk across tidal flats to Herring Cove to spend the day naked on a warm sand dune.

And the unforeseen delights of the Little Bar at the A House—tiny, dark, slate-floored, wood-fired, and juke-boxed with Ella Fitzgerald—Wellfleet oysters, scrod mornay, and a local version of bouillabaisse; live cabaret shows like Ruth Buzzi, Lily Tomlin, and Wayland Flowers and Madame, an unofficial town greeter named Charlotte—an elderly man got up like Marlene Dietrich, top hat,

cane, tights, and all—and a slew of wicked-good female imperson-
ators and campy comedians.

And there were the men. A population homogeneous in the object of their lust and love, but heterogeneous in every other way:
quick/dull, clever/pedestrian, educated/unschooled, feminine/
masculine, talented/un-, bigoted/un-, artist/laborer, and so on.

Deep-down, selfish, romantic me was disappointed that the
men weren't all handsome, buff, clever, professional, attuned to
line and hue, refined in manner and palate, liberal, and secular. But
soon, realistic me saw the strength in diversity, like the mutt's as-
cendancy over the pure-bred. Diversity, I realized, gave me a broad-
er base with which to affiliate and integrate. Diversity granted me
comfort in an extraordinary new world.

P-town was just the medicine I needed.

On my first trip to P-town I stayed at some gay guest house a
block off the main drag. By the second year I had found George and
his inn.

George had been a New York executive for ARCO, the oil company, and ditched it for the fabled life of an innkeeper in "Provin-
cialtown," as he called it. He was a short man, and quipped that
he would have been tall if God hadn't turned so much under for
feet (size 12). But his large handsome head and luxuriant black
mustache conveyed physical stature. I came to understand, also,
through subtle remarks or innuendo—George's? one or more of the
guests?—that George had a much-larger-than-average johnson. He
called it Chauncey, and word was that Chauncey's reputation lured
many a young man into the heirloom sleigh bed in a little room off
the kitchen.

George's Inn was an early sea-captain's house. The 15 or so guest
rooms didn't generate enough cash to support even a single person
in style, so management was always on the cheap. George paneled
the guest rooms with scavenged barn siding and turned Marimekko
bed sheets into draperies. He hired two college students for free
room and a pittance to clean the rooms.

Every day, in the late afternoon, happy hour descended on the lounge, after everyone had gotten back from the beach and showered. We dressed casually, tropically. Everyone drank from their own store of adult beverage. George regaled us with jokes and stories about the Inn. Guests with talent might play the piano, sing, put on short skits, or perform musical numbers. A banker from Ohio, known in P-town as Dolly, brought a trunkful of costumes every August and posed as Bette Davis, Joan Crawford, or Barbara Streisand. Happy hour was boisterous fun and a social habit that no one dared miss.

The first two years at George's, I was solo. In late 1973, John and I became a couple and from then on, for three weeks every September, P-town was the autumn elixir for both of us.

In August of '78, I went off for four months of a grand sabbatical in England, to share my research on information services with library school students and faculty and library staffs around the country and amuse them with my American accent. I fancied that John would be so depressed with my absence that he would skip that September in Provincetown.

It turned out that he wasn't all that depressed: he went for the full three weeks. And it became the September When—when George called on John to help at the Inn after the usual hires went back to college; when John said yes; when John thereafter was— and *we*, starting the next year, thereafter were—September maids. We began leading two lives—for 11 months of the year, regulation-style professors; for three weeks in September, toilet-scrubbing, dust-chasing, sheet-flipping grunts in a gay guest house in return for a free room and ten bucks a week.

Our September elixir was all the more delectable for its work so opposite from professoring and for its clandestinity. We didn't breathe a word of it to any but our gay acquaintances. But then, neither of us had come out to any straight person yet.

Somewhere around 1980 or 81, we were sitting with friends in their pool outside Philadelphia, preparing for dinner by way of gin and celery sticks. Jackie, a colleague at Drexel, and Elliott, her neurologist husband, informed us that they were heading to the Cape in September, and "aren't you going to be there, and wouldn't it be great to get together for dinner? We can pick you up at your motel and blah blah and so forth."

Pick us up at George's Inn? *Gay* George's Inn?

Were we about to be outed? Was that third source of unease, societal acceptance, about to be tested?

After a few hems and haws, one or the other of us rasped, "Well, that *would* be fun! We stay at a place on Windsor Street. George's Inn. It's gay."

"What?"

"It's gay. The Inn is gay." The Inn was gay; we were not, right? But they saw the truth and seemed unfazed. Their expressions seemed to say "So what? And ...?"

So we took the next step: "We're maids there."

"Oh."

We weren't quite sure how to take their "oh," but it didn't seem negative, and the planning continued.

September arrived bearing the day for our dinner date. John and I were in the lounge at George's inn with everyone else. Cocktail hour was at full throttle—joking, bantering, laughing, singing at the piano. It happened that no one was in drag. Precisely on time, Jackie and Elliott rang the doorbell, and a guest standing near the door let them in. Eyes panned to our obviously straight and overdressed friends, and silence erupted. Elliott was literally straight, like a ramrod in a coat and tie, shoulders back. Jackie, in a smart cocktail dress, stood quivering, not like a lab that can't wait to lick your ear, but like a child just shoved out onto a stage.

They were verklempt, and John and I were close to it.

He and I edged toward the door as we galloped through introductions: "George-everybody-these-are-our-friends-Jackie-and-Elliott-we're-late-for-dinner-see ya-bye." The four of us charged out the door and down the steps, little cartoon clouds of dust puffing out of our heels.

Toward the bottom of the hill, four pairs of feet decelerated and four pairs of shoulders relaxed. We blended with the throngs on the way to their respective dinners.

"It was really nice to finally meet George," said Elliott, at last.

"What a lovely place the Inn is," said Jackie. "Aren't you lucky to be able to spend September here."

At the restaurant we feasted on fish and wine and caught up on each others' vacations and planned a lunch by their pool when we were all back in Philadelphia. Overhead, the Fates were circling, guffawing over how well they had put us through the Wringer of Awkward Circumstances. But John and I didn't hear them. Jackie and Elliott had sacrificed themselves to the Wringer for us and had come out the other side intact, still our friends. They, the first of any, had blessed our sexual definition and approved our extraordinary September sojourn. They had granted us the third comfort—comfort with at least a small portion of the outside, heterosexual world.

14

Anti-Climax

A skirmish with pornography in my first teaching gig.

"69" named not only the year but, in the sexual explorations of the day, a revolutionary formation of two bodies for sex. In June of that year I drove my brand new copper-colored Plymouth Duster from Rutgers to Syracuse University, to my first teaching job.

After interviewing for faculty positions at Syracuse and Drexel, I had opted for the excitement of the rebirth of the Drexel school and of a city more cosmopolitan than Syracuse, NY. To maintain an open door with the Syracuse school, I agreed to help them out by teaching for the hard-to-staff summer term, when the regular faculty tend to evaporate into vacations or research projects.

The previous November, on my first trip to Syracuse, I was impressed with that charming slice of early-twentieth-century apple pie, like the set of *Meet Me In Saint Louis* with "Seventy-Six Trombones" playing up and down the square—as postcard a main street and hometown as you could find. It was a Norman Rockwell painting, with panoramas of clapboard Victorian houses and mature American elms. The trees' November silhouettes—hundreds of them—rose up tall and arched over houses and streets, raising the cityscape to elegance the way a high-ceilinged room does an interior. They promised broad green canopies floating overhead in the summer.

In June, I returned for the summer teaching in my little Duster. It was a Magritte landscape: the elms stately but still bare, as in December, while all round was green June. They were dead—Dutch Elm Disease DED. They had succumbed all at once, it seemed. The city couldn't take their cadavers down fast enough, and limbs were snapping off like zombies' arms and clattering down on cars and sidewalks and citizens.

* * *

The dean at Syracuse assigned me two courses: Quantitative Methods, a course in basic statistical methods and survey research—fully-syllabused and minutely archived, thank goodness; and Mass Media of Communication—undefined and void of any documentation. This course was to be the major time-sink for my summer.

The readings I assigned for Mass Media led us early in the course to intellectual freedom. Librarians and their American Library Association have long been among the staunchest defenders of intellectual freedom in the world. For a library school to be accredited by the ALA it must teach intellectual freedom, and Syracuse's catalog guaranteed that the Mass Media course would cover it.

Intellectual freedom is as subtle and ambiguous as all the greys in the Benjamin Moore chipbook: an illusion, teetering on a pedestal of rhetoric that is built and rebuilt every time it's debated. It could be a real Chimera, fire-breath and all, for a teacher to try to lead students through its maze of argument and opinion.

The students were all graduate students, mature and bright. Their discussion of IF was lively and polite. But such interchanges eventually reveal the vexing weaknesses of the purist IF argument, by bringing out the demons of prejudice, topics so loathsome that we would consign them to a communication dungeon, if we could, where they would never see the light of day—like instructions on how to commit suicide or build a bomb, tutorials in seducing children, tracts favoring racial bigotry, pamphlets on totalitarianism, or arguments for genital mutilation, for unlimited gun control, for fundamentalist religion, against fundamentalist religion.

But the professional position for librarians remains: utter freedom of information, at least for adults.

At that time, in the era of the sexual revolution, courses like Mass Media raised the issue of pornography—less virulent than many of the demon topics—as a test of a true IF believer: How would you address a patron's request for a pornographic document or for referral to somewhere to acquire same? (The issue then was not complicated by the matter of exploitation of porn actors or of women's rights. It was mainly about society's stomach for tolerating it.)

I had a small collection of underground newspapers, starting with the *Village Voice* when it was considered underground, and proceeding through *Screw* magazine and an assortment of mags and rags that ranged from erotic to soft porn to turgid porn. I brought it to class one day and did a brief show-and-tell. I asked how many of the class had been exposed to hard-core pornography. Few raised their hands. Vera was one of them.

Vera was a perky bottle blond who liked to dress her fireplug figure in yellow. Younger than most of the class, she was going straight from baccalaureate to the Master of Library Science degree. She stopped me after class. "I know someone who can get me a 16mm sex film, if you'd like to show it in class." Next meeting, I asked if the class would want to see a bit of porn. They voted for it unanimously—even the two middle-aged women in grey-blue nun's garb who drove a 150 miles round trip from a remote convent.

The next week, we pulled the shades, turned off the lights, and loaded the film into the projector. With the press of the "on" button, it took off to a constant metallic churning sound punctuated with rattles, scrapes, and whistles.

The film had no title or other credits, just jerky frames of a man and a woman in wavering light engaged in standard missionary-style intercourse. No foreplay, no post-coital cigarette; just in-and-out pistoning. Black and white, grainy and very close up. Sometimes I couldn't tell what body part was doing what to which other body part. It was soundless, aside from the grumbling of the projector. Class members filled in with lame and nervous little jokes and giggles, also nervous. It was over in 7 minutes. I ran it again. The jokes got better and fewer, and the giggles turned genuine: now it was boring. The students claimed to have been desensitized, at least somewhat—beginning to set aside personal twinges, objectifying this controversial area of information.

It got better. A few days later, I learned of a professor in the communications department who specialized in erotic visual material and shopped a slide-show talk on erotic art all over the country. I talked him into presenting a university-wide lecture featuring his seamy slides, sponsored by my Mass Media class and the library school. The class thrilled to the idea, and the Dean was pleased with the publicity the event would bring to the school.

Early one Thursday evening, students and faculty from all walks of academic life packed a large campus auditorium to experience "A Slide-Lecture on Erotic Art through the Ages."

Professor X—so-called here not to protect him, but because I don't remember his name and, coincidentally, his speciality was X-rated—took the stage. He began with slides of ancient-to-old art that were more suggestive than pornographic: the jiggly bits were under cloth or behind props, and the most prurient showed a hand suggestively positioned under another's clothing or one's own. The slides became more current and the people less clothed, and eventually they were wearing nothing but loin cloths. Their poses were more titillating and erotic. The slides moved into the modern era—where mere bare female bosoms gave way to full-frontal nudity. It was here, when historic progression brought the good professor to eroticism when no holds were barred, that he barred his holds. He had overlaid the reproductive organs in the artworks with fig leaf drawings; on slides that depicted insertion of one body part into another, the fig leaves were larger, as there were multiple organs to cover.

The program ran its course. There was a hum in the audience. In the following Q and A, people raised some academic and historical points, but the ones that defined the evening were about the fig leaves. Several people wondered in various wordings why the show went Puritanical when penises and vaginas were on parade. Didn't this take us in the wrong direction? Weren't the bowdlerized slides perpetuating censorship, caving in to the delimiters of intellectual freedom? Professor X had no answer. He seemed abashed.

The audience dispersed into the summer evening. Disappointment, frustration, maybe anger hung on the humid air. The audience was probably no more intellectually free than when they arrived.

I recalled the skeletons of the elm trees of Syracuse—their graceful November stalks fraudulently promising the green parasols of summer, but not delivering, like Professor X. For our class of 14 or so brave souls, their big moment—to extend their own enlightenment to the larger community—turned out to be coitus interruptus.

15

At Last

Love comes finally to this otherwise clueless one, who then frets and farts his way through a pre-booked Christmas in England.

The autumn of 1973 did not promise to be any different for me from the innumerable autumns preceding: loveless. My Boswell—if I had had one—would have pored over my journals—if I had kept any—in vain to find more amour in my thirty-fourth year than in my previous thirty-three.

He would have found two near-crushes on girls when I was an undergraduate; an infatuation in my late twenties with a tall young man that my lovelorn state trumped up into "love"; and, later, an exploratory affair with another man, which failed in short order when he disappeared in a deep depression.

Bozzy would eventually have found a pivotal entry in my would-be diary in the summer of 1973 to the effect that I had resigned myself to the single life.

Maybe forsaking romance opened me up for it a few months later. My decision to live the life of a happy singleton may have stripped off an aura of desperation that repelled potential love objects, or may have unveiled to me a wider range of possibilities.

Or maybe life's ironic penchant led me to take on the mantle of eternal singleness at the very moment when fate was slicking down Eros's sideburns from behind and getting ready to propel him with a Birkenstock to the butt through the doorway of my life.

Or maybe it was just that Mr. Right happened along at that point and made the season what it turned out to be.

Whatever the explanation, the season brought love. And a true irony came with it: I had committed to a trip abroad—tickets paid for, all arrangements made. It was a brag-worthy vacation and, at any other time, I would have been vibrating with anticipation. But now that love was in sight, the trip was a speed bump, of the five-mile-an-hour variety. And just under the paving lay the anxiety that my new beau and his current partner weren't exes yet, and that three weeks apart—beau and me—would be ample time for their flame to rekindle.

The stimuli for the trip—a Christmas vacation—were Toni and David. They moved to Philadelphia from Brown University, newly married and BAs in hand—Toni to get her master's in information studies at Drexel and David his PhD in the philosophy of science at Penn. I was an assistant professor of information studies at Drexel. Maybe because Toni and I were about the same age and the three of us loved to cook, we quickly became friends. Toni finished her program in less than a year. About the time she was walking up the aisle to accept her diploma from the Dean's hand, David was opening an envelope with news that, for no particular reason and without application, he had been granted a generous sum from Brown to live in Europe for a year. No obligations—just live in Europe.

In September, just before he and Toni flew off to live in England, they begged me to visit for a few weeks. What's to beg? My maiden trip to England, two good friends, and free housing? So I put down hard money for the airfare. As I was tucking the credit card back into my wallet, romance came calling.

* * *

Two years earlier, I was on the committee that recommended that the College hire John. He filled a niche on the faculty nicely. He seemed a regular guy and got along well with everyone, including me. The dean even assigned us to share a hotel room on two faculty retreats in Ocean City. We got acquainted to a superficial, collegial degree. Nothing deep or personal.

After the second faculty retreat, in the fall of '73, as John began his second year, a friend of his from Tallahassee came to Drexel to get his master's in information studies. Ken was uber-gay. He managed to visit all the gay bars in Philadelphia at least once in his first week, including one near my apartment, on Spruce Street. I happened to be having a nightcap when he popped in.

The next Saturday evening at the same bar, I was nursing a beer. Ken walked in, John in tow. It wasn't a great leap to assume that John was gay.

A couple of Saturdays later, John drove in from his apartment in the far burbs to go bar-hopping with me. We went to Steps, a plush new gay lounge, and had some beers and talked till final call put us out on the street. I asked which way he was parked. He pointed left and said, "That way." He asked where my apartment was, and I pointed right and said, "That way." We shook hands goodnight, he turned left, and I turned right. By the middle of the turn, my brain was screaming, "Oh, shit!"

The next morning I called him and apologized for not asking him to the apartment for a drink and maybe a stay-over so he wouldn't have that long drive back (yeah, right). He invited me to his apartment for dinner that evening. I took the train out to Glen Riddle. He introduced me to his cat, Maude. We marveled that we had each bought the latest Morgana King album the day before. He fed me chicken breast stuffed with ham. I stayed the night.

We started dating, and in short order, we rarely spent a night apart.

So there I was, in love. Staring slack-jawed out my office window at John's mirage in the middle distance and reveling in a passion that stupefied me with its novelty and intensity, brought my concentration to a halt a dozen times before lunch, befuddled my sentences in public, and twisted my guts into an inward smile from the surety that my love was like no other's, ever, and the certainty that This. Is. It.

But irony called. I had to go to England. I couldn't tell Toni and David what was up, because I'd have to divulge who was the object of my affection, and I wasn't out and open enough to do that. Actually, I wasn't out at all. So I went, carrying in my addled head an endless loop of Etta Jones crooning, "At last, my love has come along, My lonely days are over, And life is like a song...."

* * *

The cottage that Toni and David have rented is near Saffron Walden, a market village northeast of London, pretty far from any large civilization. The cottage is English Charming, of the kind with ancient ruddy-brick walls and bona-fide thatched roof, tiny kitchen appliances and rude plumbing, white picket fence and baby rabbits in a front yard that should have a charming English perennial garden but doesn't. The living-dining room, kitchen, and bathroom are on the first floor. Three small bedrooms are on the second. As I awake the first morning, sparrows are chirpily pulling straws out of the thatch over my head.

The refrigerator is the size of a modest clothes hamper and the weather isn't reliably cold enough to store perishables outside, so we're forced to market daily. Toni and I buckle ourselves into their tiny beat-up Morris Minor. David, at the front of the car, cranks till it turns over, jumps in, and drives us off to wherever.

The village farmer's market is exotic to the extent that it offers some items that we don't often find in markets in 1973 United States—such as streaky bacon, leeks, and fresh rabbit, pheasant and quail and other local vegetables.

Many days we drive around the high-grassed flatlands of East Anglia, where sailboats cruise absurdly along narrow waterways between banks of tall grasses. At Cambridge University we hear Christmas carols in the cathedral of King's College. Further north, we try to absorb the gigantic Ely Cathedral.

Several times we follow public footpaths on a daytime pub crawl, up hill and down dale, our boots squelching field mud, heavier with every step as we race to the next pub before we have to use the loo, and lunching in the farthest pub on English cheeses, bread, butter, Scotch eggs, cold pork pies, and the odd shepherd's pie. One day we pass a hog larger than the Morris Minor, its grey-bristled spine about 5 feet off the ground.

We train to London for a few days and stay with David's parents in their town house behind Buckingham Palace. His mother makes us kippered herring in the coffee percolator for breakfast. We do London's major parks, department stores, and museums, and seek solace in some delicious pub food at the Salisbury, in the theater district.

But I am elsewhere. There's always an otherness in my mind, as if I'm being whispered to from another room. An emptiness under my sternum, like being hungry, but of the spirit, not the stomach. A vapor. It is about John, of course. I would like to phone, despite the cost. I would like to send a letter or postcard every day. But communications would tip my hand and out me.

Back in Saffron Walden, the country routine resumes. The only restaurants in driving distance serve stereotypically bad English food, so we eat dinners at home. Being as it's winter and we're in an English cottage made cozy with a blazing fire, we read the Hobbit to each other. David has made some good beer, which magnifies the glow of the fire, the digestion, and Tolkien's sweet-flowing, archaic prose. The coziness is fully saturated.

Christmas approaches. In the side yard we find a Charlie Brown cedar tree: short, skinny, scant branches. We dig it up in a ball of dirt so we can replant it later. Toni and I make ornaments out of paper, aluminum foil, popcorn and cuttings from magazines.

Christmas in an English hamlet evokes the Scrooge cliché, which evokes the Christmas goose cliché. The Saturday before Christmas we seek out a cliché big enough to feed three people.

First, the poulterer is astounded that these crazy Americans want a goose, while all the natives will be eating turkey. Second, he allows as how the smallest bird he would butcher would weigh about eight pounds—too big and too expensive. But we order it anyhow.

On the morning of Christmas eve, we pick up the bird, Brussels sprouts, some things called Jerusalem artichokes, a mince pie for dessert, something or other for the Christmas eve dinner that night, and pastries for breakfast. The goose fits in the refrigerator only by itself. Luckily, it's turned cold, so all the other perishables can survive in the trunk of the Morris Minor.

Christmas morning we get up late, light a fire, gather round the Charlie Brown Christmas tree, and exchange small presents over pastries and coffee. Eventually we turn to constructing the main meal. The Brussels sprouts get steamed and their cream sauce made. The Jerusalem artichokes are peeled and parboiled, ready for the oven. The cream is whipped for the pie and set outdoors under an inverted flowerpot.

The roasting pan that fits the goose is too large for the oven, and the one that fits the oven is too small for the goose. The goose is, in fact, longer than the oven is deep. Our goose is cooked, ha ha—well not quite. We stand the bird in the smaller roasting pan and lean it diagonally across the oven. It roasts happily and throws off pints of fat. Hours later, it comes out of the oven for its final rest, and the Jerusalem artichokes go in to finish in a little goose fat.

The sun sets. The sprouts are bowled and sauced. The carved bird is laid out in golden bisymmetry. The Jerusalem artichokes cast off a curl of steam. The cranberry jelly quivers. Never was a Christmas dinner as splendid as this one, in our shire cottage.

Once sated, we retire to the fireplace with the Hobbit and brandy. Frodo and friends have moved their hairy feet barely a hundred cubits, when the Jerusalem artichokes strike.

Known by many names—sunchoke, sunroot, earth apple—but unknown to us in 1973, they contain a hyper-dose of a carbohydrate fiber, inulin. It's hard to digest and can cause gastric upset and flatulence. *Gerard's Herbal* of 1621 A.D. quotes the English planter John Goodyer: "which way soever they be dressed and eaten, they stir and cause a filthy loathsome stinking wind within the body, thereby causing the belly to be pained and tormented, and are a meat more fit for swine than men." [1]

Silently, a filthy loathsome stinking wind does arise in the room. Denial, also, is widespread in the room; without a word, we slink off to separate rooms to "read"—that is, to quietly fart—the evening away.

* * *

I endured my wistful but priceless holiday. I came away with a headful of rich memories, despite all the longing to be somewhere else. Maybe the poignancy of every moment away from John made the moments stick. Maybe the aura of first love amped up my receptors. Maybe recounting every image, every adventure to John as soon as I got back fixed them securely in my brain.

At any rate, a few days after Christmas, I return to John, full of relief to be with him, and full of stories. When he meets me at the Philadelphia airport, I'm carrying an antique railway clock wrapped in newspaper—a gift to me, I guess, because we're not quite "us." For him I bring an antique water carafe and a set of art nouveau egg cups, which John receives graciously, even though I know as I hand them over that they are too insignificant, too guarded a present.

By New Year's day we have become "us." John has terminated the relationship with his former partner, and we are free. Still high in the stratosphere of new love, we set off to buy a house.

---

[1] Cited in Davidson A. (1999). *The Oxford Companion to Food,* first edition. Oxford University Press.

NOT IN OHIO ANYMORE

16

Valhalla on a Dime

A trophy family vacation puffs up my status among the peers,
but ultimately seals my academic fate.

They weren't secretive, as a rule. But Mom and Dad went underground with any topic with a scent of money. Sometime in the late winter of 1954, they must have been conferring privately, for one weekend at the dinner table, they announced to my younger brother and me that the family was going to Washington, DC.

There was no practical reason to go to Washington, DC. We didn't have relatives there; they were all in Ohio, like us, or West Virginia. We didn't have friends in DC, either, and Dad had no work affiliates there. The going to Washington had to be: VACATION!—that fabled, unhoped-for getaway, that respite from the diurnal, the ho-hum, the stultifying familiarity of our puny lives in small-town Ohio.

Mom and Dad maintained that tromping around the heart of the republic would prepare us boys for a richer school experience and give us a broad world view that would serve us all our lives. They didn't put it in those terms, exactly, but the message was conveyed. Indeed, neither of us had gotten further outside the Ohio borders than very northern West Virginia, just across the Ohio River. To my thinking, my little brother, at 11, didn't yet have a mind ready for enriching or a world view worth broadening. Mom and Dad's message had to be directed at me, just turned 14 and about to enter senior high school. It was one of those moments when I felt I was being deliberately raised, and I felt honored.

Pedagogical motives aside, Dick and I knew there would also be adventure in the trip. But even more valued by us was the fact that the DC gambit would put my brother and me in the elite class of our peers who took vacations.

A couple of weeks later, certainly after more clandestine collusion, Mom and Dad gathered us for a vacation update. Dad allowed as how we might, if we were temperate, stoic, parsimonious, and lucky, go further than DC. We might even get to Florida.

Holy moly. My brother and I were flabbergasted. This was an exponential escalation, into the promised land of sunny skies, crystal waters, tall pink birds, man-eating plants, alligator wrestling, philodendrons as big as Cadillacs, walking catfish, deadly swamps, elixirs of youth, poisonous frogs, and other unbelievably cool things. In the mid-50s, to a family in the northern tier of the country, Florida—this exotic, erotic land of tropical humidity, salty seas, hibiscus stamens, and the breath of orange blossoms on every tongue—was a magnetic direction not to be reckoned with: True South.

Setting Florida as our vacation target thrust us into the privileged class. Surely, returning to school in September, I would be pleasantly torn between the overt and the subtle: approaching my classmates and informing them that I'd just come back from Florida, or letting my mahogany suntan and sun-bleached hair do the talking. I was sure that my parents, too, looked forward to suppressing their own smugness as they recounted the trip to friends and peers—not just keeping up with the Joneses, as they would have done with a DC vacation, but surpassing them and keeping up with the, well, the Rockefellers.

Immediately after the Florida Escalation, Mom and Dad got serious and impressed on us that it would be a vacation on a budget—

pinching the penny in every way possible. I had always been aware of the family's slender means and was accustomed to sacrifice in order to have, say, a six-pack of Royal Crown Cola for the weekend. And I'd always earned money at something, it seemed, from helping clean classrooms after school in the fifth grade, to mowing lawns, to delivering newspapers. So it was no stretch for me to sign on to penny-pinching. My brother, who hadn't yet started making any money, wasn't in any position to object to budgetary constraints.

Because of Dad's work schedule, we had to put the trip off to the very end of August, which meant I'd be two days late registering for my freshman courses. Mr. J.A. Smith, the principal for 40 years—ramrod straight, white hair parted in the middle, black-suited, detachable-collared—was not known for flexibility. He refused my parents' request to let me register early. But he did grant us two days grace in registering. The agreement had the ring of victory to my parents and me. We had no inkling that the ring might be hollow.

Our car was just purchased, and brand new—an historic first for our family. It was a pale green Dodge, four doored and un-air-conditioned (what car was, in those days?). Newness notwithstanding, the car came with a built-in flaw that could have vacated the vacation: a couple of weeks before our ETD, Dad discovered an oil leak. Diagnostics showed that faulty casting had left the differential housing with a pinhole leak. Sadie, as Dad called all his cars, was not a well car. There wasn't time to install a new differential housing before we left. Dad took the leap and decided that Sadie could cover 4,000 miles if he monitored her fluid levels along the way. The car dealership would give us a little cash back and replace the housing when we returned.

So we set off down US Route 23 to Florida. We went by way of the Great Smokey Mountains.

The US interstate highway system was still being dreamed up, so our pace was slow. Highways were two lanes—one each way—and speed limits were 45 to 50 mph at best. When we hit the Smokies, with its narrow ridges and switchbacks and absence of guard rails, the limits were even lower. But it gave us time to absorb the vertical mountain greenery, mock the misuse of apostrophes on hand-lettered signs ("coon pup's cheap"), and toy with buying a white chenille bedspread or a Native-American craft from the heaps of beaded moccasins, beaded-leather pouches, beaded tomahawks, and chicken-feathered headdresses.

At some point, as Sadie twisted and turned through West Virginia, Kentucky and Tennessee, I noticed that we were going much slower than the speed limit and realized, without his saying anything, that those high, winding roads had brought out a serious case of acrophobia in my father. His white knuckles regained their color and he started exhaling regularly only when he brought us down onto the relatively flat terrain that would carry us through to mythic Florida.

There was a lot of car time. We wiled away the miles conversing, trying to find radio stations that weren't country music or tent revival, and gazing silently at the new land: tiny towns and villages, shacks moldering in the middle of sun-burnt pastures, fields without fences, cows without fences, highways without shoulders. And reading Burma Shave ditties on rows of tiny sequential billboards ("Train approaching / Whistle squealing / Stop / Avoid that run-down feeling / Burma-Shave"). My brother and I—assigned to the back seat on either side of a picnic basket—must have spent some of our time aggravating each other, but I don't remember specifics and don't remember being yelled at by the folks. He and I sometimes played "bing"—seeing who could spot a cow first—till the cows got so populous that there wasn't any point in it. Now and then, the whole family would tally license plates from the various states.

We ate on the cheap. In 1954, American cheese was 55 cents a pound; bread was 17 cents a loaf; Grape Nuts cereal was 19 cents for 10 ounces. In Georgia, men in a field were selling watermelons, warm right out of the field, at twenty-five cents for ten; we bought one for a nickel and ate it beside the road. Mom cobbled together breakfast in our motel room (bread, butter, jam, bananas). For lunch, we'd often stop at a grocery store for sandwich fixings, then stop outside town, throw open the car doors, and picnic beside the highway. We were always on the lookout for ice to provision the cooler chest on the back floor.

Our preferred mode of dinner, defined by budget and outdoor fun, was a city park. We would invade a grocery store for provisions, find a city park, and cook our meal on a public grill, if there was one, or on the little hibachi that Mom had packed. A couple of times, when Mom and Dad deemed the family coffers robust enough, we sat down in an actual restaurant—modest, to be sure—for dinner. Mom popped the leftover bread and packs of crackers into her purse.

We slept on the cheap, too. About 4 p.m. every evening we'd start scouting for a motel. Holiday Inns and their ilk were too pricey; but there were plenty of cheap ones, from $5 to $10 a night, and most of them clean. Dick and I always begged for a motel with pool, and now and then Mom and Dad coughed up the extra dollar.

It took three days and two nights to reach Valhalla. We touched down in Panama City. It was a shabby-shack town back then and easy to find a cheap motel right on the Gulf of Mexico. The water was no more than ankle-deep, no matter how far out we waded, awash in palm and coconut debris, as waveless as plate glass and as warm as fresh piss.

Not Valhalla yet.

Things improved as we cut diagonally across the state toward Miami and sampled fabled tourist attractions: the mermaids of Weeki Watchee Springs; the storied road outside Lake Wales, where your car looks as if it's rolling uphill; the crystal depths of Silver Springs seen through a glass-bottom boat; the birds and plants of the original Busch Gardens; innumerable Stuckeys gift shops when we stopped for gas (21 cents a gallon). We took pleasure in all of them, intrinsically and, more important, stored up material for the tales we'd tell up north.

Eventually, we found ourselves in Miami. Starting at the south end of Miami Beach, Dad drove us slowly north, as we gaped at the gargantuan hotels on the glistening sands—palaces of the wealthy, taller than any buildings we had ever seen, where uniformed door-men unloaded families in white linens from the likes of Bentleys and Rolls Royces (which we didn't yet know enough to name). One palace, about to take its place in history, the Fontainebleau, was brand new.

In our pale green Dodge, with cooler in the back seat and the hibachi in the trunk, we felt poor and hickish for the first time on this trip—not quite white trash, but certainly less privileged than before we hit the glittering shores of southern Florida. At least I did. Maybe Mom, Dad, and Dick were awed enough or un-self-con-scious enough to be spared the feeling.

At any rate, Miami had no affordable accommodations and maybe not even affordable baloney or bananas. So we continued on up the coast till we got to Daytona Beach. There we set our feet in the Atlantic Ocean for the first time and pounded our feet on the hard-packed white beach. The pristine water, the vigor of the waves, the chill of the surf were a new world. A couple of blocks off the beach we found a small motel, where a room came with a small kitchen. Mom could cook real meals! And it was under budget! And the owner threw in the adjoining room, so for the first time on the trip my brother and I weren't in a panic to fall asleep before Dad started snoring. We stayed there several days.

Then we drove to the ancient walls of St. Augustine and from there, homeward, hugging the coast so Dad could avoid mountain driving. A couple of days later Sadie, oil-leak survivor, disgorged the family onto the sidewalk in front of our house gloating privately at having pulled off 10 days in Florida for less than $200, and eager to gloat publicly at being Florida-vacation veterans.

The next day I walked over to the high school and reported to the principal's office to register for my freshman year, two days late, as agreed. Every class required for the academic track was still available. Good. The sole Freshman elective on that track would be language, either French or Latin. Everyone I knew was going to enroll in French. And I guess they did, because the principal advised me that all the seats were taken. I threw myself on his mercy. But, stiff of back and forward of chin, he refused to squeeze one more seat into the French class, and I was stuck with Latin. Then he congratulated me on my good choice and pointed out my stellar scores on last year's Latin Affinity Estimator (or some such name).

That was when I knew I'd been had. That the vacation was a ruse. That its timing was a plot to make me late for registration and force me into Latin. That my parents were probably in on it.

In the end, I took my tanned and semi-blond and deflated self to Miss Kelhoffer's Latin I.

17

Christmas in Stir

*Tee-totaling no more, as Dad upends tradition
with red bubbly on the Christmas table.*

My father told people he took up prison work to be close to his sons. Ha ha. But in an inverted way it was true. He *did* work in prisons and, once he reached the rank of associate warden, he and his family lived on the prison grounds, as was the rule, and he was physically as close to his two sons and his wife as he was to work.

For eleven years, from the time I was 20, our family lived in stir, doing time, as it were, in quarters we were required to rent from the Federal Bureau of Prisons. Mom and Dad, of course, lived in those places full-time, along with Dagmar, our chunky black-and-white mongrel named after a 1950's blonde-bombshell TV comedienne, and my brother, Dick, till he moved on to medical school. I, in various stages of degree grubbing, unindentured servitude (Army), and commencement of career, was a sometime resident.

Even after Dick and I had left the nest, we were frequently at home, whatever prison it might be, and always for Christmas. Over the years the government-supplied home was a huge apartment on one of the highest hills in Washington, DC, a modest bungalow in California looking down on a valley of Burpee flower fields, and a sprawling ranch-style home near Denver facing the foothills of the Rockies.

The DC home was the best. It was also where Dad and his sons were closest (ha ha again), since we lived above his office. It was a large red-brick Georgian edifice commissioned by President Lincoln. The first floor housed the offices of the National Training School for Boys (euphemism for prison), where Dad, the director (euphemism for warden), and his staff worked.

Our family lived on the second floor in the same ten-room apartment that had housed the families of previous directors. Compared with our house in southern Ohio, where walls and ceilings were always close—at hand or head—these were palatial digs. The long-legged ceilings stretched off into forever; the living and dining rooms were mansion-sized, the bedrooms, family room, utility room, kitchen, and bathrooms just plain big. Working within the Bureau's allotment, Mom and an interior-decorator friend embellished on the ordinary furnishings (beds, couches, end tables, etc.) by adding brocade draperies, copies of Sheraton furniture in the dining room, and a gigantic blue sofa in the living room facing the marble fireplace 30 feet away.

The Training School was on one of the highest hills in DC. A center hall ran the length of our apartment, ending in a wrought-iron balcony. From it, you could see almost into the center of DC, beyond the massive dome of the Basilica of the National Shrine of the Immaculate Conception, which glinted far off like a single sequin. You could spread your arms and pretend to be prince of it all. Sometimes, we would stand on the balcony dressed for dinner and give the royal wave to our guests as they parked below.

From the back windows of the apartment we could see the dormitories and classrooms of the Training School. But interaction between the school and our family, except for Dad, was rare. We saw personnel or inmates as needed—when they hauled firewood up to the back door or made plumbing repairs, for instance. Otherwise, we were fully insulated from the grim realities of incarcerated youth and prison life.

(In one of life's unnumbered coincidences, Charles "Helter Skelter" Manson had been a teenage "guest" of the Training School some years before and had been transferred to the Ohio reformatory where Dad started his career, and at about that same time. Our family was ignorant of these close encounters, and I think Dad, too. We felt private and safe in our luxe aerie.)

As I was growing up, in Ohio, dining was just the four of us, unless Mom's mother or the aunt and cousin from West Virginia stayed overnight. Now and then a really local family member or two would invade our tight little family quartet for Sunday dinner—maybe Great Aunt Neva or Dad's sister's family. That would render Dad grumpy before ("When the hell are they supposed to get here?"), sullen during, and resentful after ("I thought they'd never quit saying good-bye.").

Mom and Dad would have people over to watch TV or play croquet, before or after dinner; but we rarely entertained with food. I think it was my father's strong anti-social streak. He could charm a snake, but he was, not very deep down, a curmudgeon. Everyone loved him, but he couldn't wait to be alone.

So we ate mostly by our nuclear-family selves—and adamantly at Thanksgiving and Christmas: Allen and Jeannette and Tom and Dick, and a dog if there were one, cocooned at the kitchen table, savoring a feast made all the more festive by excluding others.

Our first Christmas at the Training School was a couple of weeks away when planning began. It didn't need to be said that the day would follow our habit of exclusion. As to decoration, it was family consensus that the astounding high ceilings of the apartment deserved an astounding tall Christmas tree.

Dick and I, at the stage of life when we were infinitely more astute than our parents, struck out in the VW Beetle one evening. It was snowing, which stirred up our Christmas passions and augured well for a tree-finding adventure. An hour or so later, Mom and Dad watched from the wrought-iron balcony as a twelve-foot

Douglas fir glided, supine (or prone; it's hard to tell with a tree), up the snow-clad driveway and into Dad's parking space. The little yellow Beetle was buried underneath.

Planning for Christmas dinner was progressing when, one day, Dad revealed a treat. If he'd been the kind of man who made a big deal out of anything or held back for a surprise, he'd have said, "I've got something pretty special for Christmas dinner" and no more. Being neither of these kinds of man, he simply announced, "I got some Cold Duck for Christmas dinner."

"What's that?" Dick and I asked.

"Red wine with bubbles. You drink it cold."

* * *

That first Christmas at the Training School wasn't the first time wine had stained the family tablecloth. The inauguration took place about two years earlier, at our house in West Hyattsville, Maryland, the DC suburb where we lived when Dad was first assigned to the home office of the Bureau of Prisons. He wasn't yet at the warden level, so we were still living in a house we owned.

The dining room could seat eight. Mom had arm-wrestled some of the curmudgeonry out of Dad, and entertaining with food happened more frequently than it had back in Ohio. In a reckless burst of other-orientation, Dad, on his own, asked a fellow bureaucrat to our house for dinner. Mr. Kvernick's family was off visiting relatives in Sweden for a couple of weeks.

The main course was to be spaghetti, with Mom's own sauce. Maybe it was the Italian-ness of the menu or, maybe, the cosmopolitan influence of Washington, DC, but something inspired Dad to end prohibition in the house and serve wine. This was momentous in and of itself, but more so in the face of my father's Baptist background, which equated beer with horse piss and hard liquor with turpentine; and my mother's Christian Scientist faith, which forbade any form of alcohol.

Shortly before our guest arrived, someone discovered that we didn't own wine glasses, and Dad drove off to buy some. I was busy helping get the meal ready.

At the hour of dining, I rinsed the cooked spaghetti, and Mom plated spaghetti and sauce. Everyone was called to the table. We put fork to food. My first bite blasted me with the memory of having rinsed the pasta under cold water. I sat still, spending precious seconds reflecting on James Beard's aphorism that almost anything hot tastes better cold and concluding that it didn't apply to spaghetti. Mom, on the other hand, in a choreographed set of fluidic motions, sprang to her feet, swallowed her first cold bite, snatched Kvernvick's plate from under his fork, and ran to the kitchen, where she rinsed the leftover unsauced pasta under hot tap water, drained it, added some to the plate with more hot sauce, and shoved it back under his quivering fork. Kvernvick stared at the massively heaping plateful. You could tell he was figuring how to choke down enough to be respectful. We all knew what he was thinking, and he knew that we knew. What he didn't know yet was that it was barely warm.

While this spaghetti comedy was playing out, Dad was pouring red wine into, we finally notice, strangely short glasses. Where did Dad say he got them? At Walgreens? The drugstore Walgreens? Surely not. But surely so, for Walgreen's was close at hand, and it carried a little bit of everything. Dad, not being acquainted with the niceties, or even the grossities, of setting a table, had picked out small glass bowls on stubby feet: sherbet dishes. We were drinking our inaugural wine out of goddamn sherbert dishes.

* * *

Nor was the introduction of wine at the first Christmas at the Training School the maiden voyage of wine even in that setting. Some months earlier, Gibby, a fraternity brother of Dick's and mine, joined the family for a weekend dinner. Mom—always the cook and perhaps heady over the fact that my brother and I had a mutual friend for the first time in our lives—created a sumptuous meal. Dad made it a high occasion, too, by unveiling a bottle of wine, which in proud defiance of the law he poured for my underage brother and our friend (by this time, into proper wine glasses). All went well—the food, the wine, the conversation with handsome, charming, refined Gibby—till, as we were closing in on the dessert course, there came a fart. A fart of perfect tone and embouchure. Not a wobbly, smelly poot, but a single-toned and odorless blast of the finest kind. Nonetheless, a fart of the sort that could not be denied as the creak of a chair or the scrape of a dish across the table or a small piece of door molding hitting the floor. It was a fart, and it came from Gibby. My brother and I were so busy looking poker-faced to mask our horror and embarrassment and so focused on pretending that we didn't hear a thing, even Gibby's quiet "Excuse me," that the celebratory occasion of the wine that day was lost to us.

* * *

Finally, the first Christmas in the Training School apartment, in DC, arrived. The excitement of the new made things memorable: the huge Christmas tree in the middle of the living room between the fireplace and the couch; the view out the dining-room windows down the long snowless hill to Bladensburg Road; the mouth-watering smells wafting out of the kitchen.

Mom had covered the dining room table with red netting over red cotton yard goods. She laid out her sterling and her good china, both patterned with little flowers—frilly and very Mom. On the large wall facing the dining room window was a four-by-eight-foot still life of mammoth oranges and a big blue pitcher on blue cloth that I had painted in a Cézannoid moment a few months earlier. Wine glasses sat ready on the sideboard. (Mom, who knew by now to do it herself, had ordered them from the Blenko Glass Works in West Virginia—the very design that Jackie Kennedy had just chosen for the White House.) The dining room, most often used by Mom as an ironing room, was ready for a Christmas dinner for four.

We never had turkey at Christmas, or even Thanksgiving. None of us liked it. When I was younger, feast meals consisted of things that we couldn't afford on a daily basis, such as shrimp or lamb. Later, as the family fortunes improved, we turned to things that were extravagant or unusual, like lobster tail or beef tartare.

Today it was a twelve-inch standing rib of beef, rare, and Mom's first-ever Yorkshire pudding, throwing off salty hot-tallow smells, and Brussels sprouts with béchamel. Dad popped the cork on the First Christmas Booze: Cold Duck: icy, bubbly, and deep maroon. He poured it slowly into the genuine wine glasses. Mom, glamorous in a flowered silky dress, her fingers splayed out on the red netting as if she were drying her nails, sat quietly, abstaining as always, smiling like a Mona Lisa over our wicked pleasure. Dick, Dad, and I toasted Christmas and the indulgence of the wine and ceremoniously brought the glasses to our faces. We examined the nose, legs, and other body parts of the wine as if we knew what we were doing. We took our sips and proclaimed it "very good." We smiled, terribly pleased with ourselves and each other. A novice at wine, I still had no illusion that it was the best I would ever have, but it was without doubt better than no wine at all and far better than that for being on the family table at our very exclusive Christmas feast.

18

Saving Mr. Goodlife

Grasping for gentility in the US Army.

At 23, I already knew that life played tricks—sometimes in the form of tragedies, sometimes comedies, often ironies. In early October, 1963, irony came knocking.

I had a freshly earned master's degree, what I thought was my last dose of formal schooling. Out of school for the first time since I was four years old, I was ready to sample the Good Life. For me, The Good Life would include the structured comfort of a job and the unstructured comfort of weekends and evenings which I might fill with a little art (painting and mosaics, which I had done a bit of, and someday lithography) or learning to cook outside my family traditions. The Good Life would probably include a bit of travel—professional conferences, mostly, and a modest vacation here or there.

I had solved number one, the job part, of the Good Life by signing on as Librarian 1 with the Baltimore County Public Library, headquartered in Towson, and I had only to choose how to activate the rest of the GL.

Three months into it, irony arrived, in the form of a letter from President Kennedy. He and I were not in the habit of corresponding, so I feared the worst. "Greetings!" he wrote. That most dread word in the English language told me more than I wanted to know: I was being drafted. The message was jack-hammered in thusly: "You are hereby ordered for induction into the Armed Forces of the United States and to report at [time] on [date] for forwarding to an Armed Services Induction Station."

My new-found pen pal, the President, urged me to present myself in a few weeks to Fort Holabird, in Baltimore, and I did, where men in olive drab administered tests of mind, body, and loyalty. I aced them all and raised my hand and swore the oath, and was led in, which is to say induced, which is to say in Army speak, inducted. On the spot and incredibly, I became a soldier, Private Fucking First Class Childers. They pressed papers into my hand. "Report," they read, "for duty on the 29th of November." It was 1963.

Like the clabbering of milk, unreality began to set in.

I continued to work at the library in a trance. In the back of my brain, a count-down clock banged the seconds like a funeral drum, but in my Pollyanna lobe hovered the certainty that all this was a bad dream from which something would rescue me. Surely.

The count-down clock also cautioned me to store up Good-Life activities enough to get through what was guaranteed to be two years of Army drought. So, as often as I could, I scooted down to Washington to stay with my parents and partake with them or my friends of the polyglot food of DC (Persian, Japanese, Spanish, French, Italian, German, etc.); attend several classical concerts; revisit my favorite museums (Phillips, Corcoran, parts of the Smithsonian); show up at a couple of good-bye parties; and so on.

My last day at the library, a Friday, had to have been scripted by a crazed screenwriter conjuring up a perfect gateway to a life that was about to become unreal in the sense of hallucinatory or surreal.

Towson was overcast. I occupied myself with cleaning out my desk and returning its contents to the supply cabinet. About noon the Glassips sipping-straw factory behind the library caught fire. While it pumped a thin plume of dark grey smoke into the lowering sky, the staff laid out paper plates, napkins, and forks, and dished up cake and ice cream. The fire trucks honked and squealed their way to the burning factory. My going-away party had begun.

Then the news burst in by radio from Dallas: the President had been shot. The celebrants at my party erupted in gasps and tears and stunned silence. The radio announced his death. Any thought of farewell, dessert, or me evaporated. The library closed early and everyone went home.

On Sunday, thousands of civilians, numb from the cold and the loss, lined Pennsylvania Avenue to watch a horse-drawn caisson carry the President's body to the Capitol. Muffled drumsticks beat out a hollow, morbid tattoo. My father and I were there.

Thursday was Thanksgiving, of which I have no recollection, brain-dead from our grievous national loss of the man, loss of an era of relative American innocence, and imminent loss of my personal freedom. The next day I was bused to boot camp at Ft. Gordon, Georgia.

I'd been through Georgia a time or two, but I was civilian and free then. This time, Georgia was a tumble down a rabbit hole, and not a nice one. The Army cut my hair to the length of 220-grit sandpaper and fitted me with fatigues that were too tight and boots that made me walk funny. They forced me to exercise two times a day, twice more than I was used to, run a mile without stopping, and shoot ("fire," in their language) an M-14. They made me eat indefinable food, most of which tasted like canned gravy. The routine was bleak: up-and-at-'em before dawn, chow, physical exertion, chow, more physical exertion, chow, and early to bed.

In a nod to the Good Life, one evening halfway through boot camp our uber-sergeant handed out tickets to the post movie house where they were screening that quintessential red-blooded American film for rough, tough, Army recruits: Nelson Eddie and Jeanette MacDonald's 27-year-old *Rose Marie*. Most of us didn't last ten minutes.

In another nod to the GL, toward the end of boot camp, on the eighth or ninth weekend, Sarge issued passes. We could leave the post, but were restricted to nearby Augusta, and we had to be back by sundown. Nonetheless, it was a heady prospect, the thought of mixing with civilians. A bunch of us wandered around the little downtown and, about noon, went looking for food. The first restaurant turned us away. There were empty tables, but maybe they were reserved. The second restaurant said they were just closing. But it was the height of the lunch hour. Then I caught on: except for me, we were all African-American and, outside post boundaries, this was the time-warp of the segregated south. As northerners, my buddies and I were more mystified than incensed. We found lunch in an all-black diner.

In five months the Civil Rights Act would be enacted.

When our cadre graduated from boot camp, our duty assignments scattered us across the globe. A bunch of us who were heading more or less north were packed into a derelict passenger train that bucked and heaved its way to Chicago for two days, as we read, talked, slept sitting up, and watched ice form on the inside of the windows.

In the windy city they re-sorted us. My re-formed, ever-smaller cadre lucked onto an interlude of the Good Life: the train ride continued, but this time on sleek, new cars of the Great Northern line. Each man had his own sleeper cabin, and there were cars for dining, drinking, and observing. After the deprivations of boot camp and the deprivations anticipated in our new assignments, it was difficult not to appreciate such luxury. It was also difficult not to compare it to the last supper on death row.

We rode west for three days. Most of the trip I was in the observation car, riveted by the wild and woolly winter-white terrain of Minnesota, North Dakota, Montana, and Idaho, including the Rockies. Periodically we bisected little towns and sometimes stopped for provisions. The last night I stayed awake to watch the train's moonlit sweep up the snow-covered Cascades and, as dawn was throwing peach-colored rays at our backs, down the other side toward Seattle, between emerald-green pastures dotted with black-

and-white Holsteins under pearlescent skies.

In Seattle the GL episode ended, and a bus carried us the last hour to our final destination: Ft. Lewis, Washington.

The army didn't know what to do with me. Private Fucking First Classes with high test scores or college degrees usually landed a support slot, like company clerk, accountant, or orderly for a bird colonel. Undecided cases, including me, cooled our heels in the garrison (central support) barracks.

After a couple of days doing nothing, I moseyed over to the recreation center. A "bluebird"—a civilian Army employee dressed in blue uniform—female—was working on a mosaic table. Eventually I learned that the woman, Marie, was director of the post library. "Oh," said I, "I just got my library degree at Rutgers." "Really," she said, in the sense of "You're shitting me," but she took my name and contact information anyhow.

A couple of days later I was ordered to a Military Police unit to become company clerk. But the day after that a higher authority, whose strings had been pulled by Marie, switched my destiny to the post library, in a position as librarian.

Thus I served my country, in non-combat mode, deployed and employed like a civilian, and that part of army life seemed real and Good. But in the non-work hours the unreal—sleeping in a barracks, enduring regular physical training and snap inspections, requalifying regularly in marksmanship, saluting three quarters of the people on the base, dressing in ill-fitting olive-drab fatigues, and eating in a place that smelled of grease and grease-cutting soap that was called, eponymously, a mess hall—proclaimed itself. As the days wore on, and the unreal threatened to become real, every resistant draftee, including me, fixated on moments and acts that assured him that whatever he defined as his good life was alive and kicking. Many of them, for starters, kept a count-down calendar that they ticked off every morning; I found that too focused on the depressing reality of servitude. Others corresponded interminably with friends and family back home. Others spent every cent they earned to rent a tiny apartment off base. Others vegetated in front of sports television.

At the time, Ft. Lewis was counted as the third largest city in the state; so it was natural for it to have a public library. There was the main library and two branches, staffed by six professional or semi-professional librarians and a couple of assistants. Before I joined them, the staff was civilian, female, all bluebirds.

After a few months, Marie assigned me to run the North Fort branch. As branch head, I was required to participate in monthly book selection meetings. A driver would chauffeur four of us to a warehouse in Seattle where we would select and order our books as fast as we could. This professional activity alone made it a Good-Life day. But the Good Life took a giant step when we stepped through Trader Vic's doors, to lunch as one cannot in a mess hall—on, say, a wedge of pressed chicken with crushed almonds and salad with the original green goddess dressing—and when we later shopped the food stalls of Pike Place Market to pick up snacks for the trip back to the base and, for the bluebirds, other foodstuffs for their homes.

Outside the library workday, I made friends with another Private Fucking First Class from back east. James Leo Flanigan III liked wine, women, and song (mostly folk) and a lot of what I looked for in the Good Life—like good conversation, liberal politics, secular philosophy, and good reading. He abhorred the army more than anyone I knew—so much so that he never talked about his job and I only remember that he was a company clerk somewhere. He had an old Triumph II that he drove like a Nascar racer, in contrast to my very used 1957 MG, which I drove like a chauffeur.

Flanigan was a saint to me. He engineered several Good-Life diversions that included lucky me. A common one was to drive up to Seattle for food and bars. On one extravagant diversion we booked into one of Seattle's highest-end restaurants, Canlis. It was my first haute-cuisine meal ever, and Flanigan's, too. The idea of veal kidneys in mustard sauce with black olives inflamed my young mental taste buds. I ordered it and was so not sorry. I don't remember what

Flanigan got. Such little trips helped pass many weekends in civilian similitude.

Flanigan's piece de resistance of Good-Lifery was a two-week leave in '65. We had little money, so he engineered the trip using "hops"—free military flights on a space-available basis—and military hotels for a dollar a night.

On the first leg, we hopped a twin-prop plane, swinging for four hours in canvas sling seats in its bare metal belly down to San Francisco. The flight was military; when we checked into the Marine Memorial Hotel, it was military. The city, on the other hand, was nothing but the real and the good. For a week we ate, drank, and sightsaw all over town. On plush red banquets at Ernie's we ate chicken in champagne and souffléed omelet on a puddle of creme Anglaise while tuxedoed waiters made sure to cover the dirty ashtray before swapping it for a new one. We drank Irish coffee at the Buena Vista Café by the Bay. We brunched in the glass conservatory of the Sheraton Palace Garden. We wandered under the eucalyptuses in Golden Gate Park and drank cocktails at dusk and watched lights blink on around the Bay at The Top of the Mark in the Mark Hopkins Hotel.

From San Francisco we hopped to Honolulu and little Ft. DeRussy a few yards from Waikiki Beach, where we bunked, again for a dollar a night. We swam and surfed and Jeeped around Oahu. Food wasn't memorable, except for a church luau that I remembered for the blandness of its pit-cooked pig, fruit steamed in banana leaves, and two-finger poi. But it was Good-Life quality, nonetheless: that is, it wasn't in a mess hall.

Flanigan also engineered a trip of a different kind. Frank Zappa was a co-draftee and stationed at Ft. Lewis, and Flanigan knew him, probably through his (Flanigan's) guitar-picking. Zappa confided that morning-glory seeds could produce a pleasant high; he and his girlfriend made pasta out of them and tripped regularly.

At a hardware store off-base, we bought a dozen packets of morning-glory seeds. The labels read "Not for Human Consumption." We checked into the North Fort movie house, where *Cat Ballou* was playing, and ate the seeds like popcorn. That night I had vivid dreams of penguins in tuxedoes and battleship catamaran hulls cutting through high seas. All Flanigan got was an upset stomach, and he was furious.

Soon after, he rapturously signed his discharge papers and returned to his home in Philadelphia, leaving me to wait out my final months. The war in Vietnam began to escalate. A couple of my buddies had months or a year added to their draft and were sent over. My waiting became desperate.

But the day of discharge arrived. As an anonymous lifer in olive drab pressed those blessed papers into my palm, I couldn't stop smiling. I also couldn't think of an important enough way to celebrate; so I just packed my minimal civvies and got the next plane east—laying over in Minneapolis, where an erstwhile Army buddy's parents welcomed me officially to the real and permanent Good Life by feeding me shad roe and bacon and champagne for breakfast.

Within two weeks I was back on the job in Baltimore, driving a newer sports car (TR4) in my first ever Harris-tweed sport coat, ticketed for Turandot at the Baltimore Lyric Opera House, and about to jump headlong into *Mastering the Art of French Cooking*.

Thus I won the war.

19

Le Canal du Plaisir

Cruising a canal in southwest France with no agenda more demanding than being there.

It's a slim tan ribbon, gently percolating between berms of sometimes packed earth and sometimes waving grasses, on its way from the Atlantic to the Mediterranean.

We were supposed to start the cruise in Toulouse. But the drought had dried up the 60 miles of canal south of Toulouse so, diverted downstream, John and I stood on the bank of the canal, in tiny Trebes. We were feeling a little put out, but not by the loss of 60 miles of cruising. It was the canal. Rather than a sparkling blue waterway, it looked like a puny brown drainage ditch. And the boat: while we knew that our vessel wouldn't be a long-hulled wooden barge with chef and servants, we had expected something with more character than the blue plastic throw-away craft bobbing in front of us.

The two of us had done France a couple of times, although not to the point of actual doneness. Then along came friends Carolyn and Belver, proposing a self-barging trip in France. The words were barely formed on their lips when we shouted "Oui," signing on in total ignorance—of the canal, of what self-barging meant for sure, and of how to drive-sail-whatever a boat, if self-barging meant—as it seemed to—doing it ourselves.

But we were confident. Belver, aside from being a faculty colleague of John and mine (an information scientist) had been a sailor since he was wearing Pampers, in Hampton, VA. And Carolyn, a blond beauty from an Illinois farm—art history major, turned information systems analyst at our college, turned friend of John and me, turned wife of Belver—had amateur sailor status. John and I often crewed on their sailboat on the Chesapeake, where Belver taught us some sailing things, which included referring to him as "The Great Captain."

So here we were, on the banks of the storied Canal du Midi.

> *The Romans had contemplated doing it, but never did. In the 17th century, Pierre-Paul Riquet made it his major life work; and when it opened in 1681, a few years after he died, the Canal du Midi provided a short and pirate-free passage across a rugged corner of France, from the Atlantic to the Mediterranean. A marvel of engineering then and now, it strikes awe again and again for its many locks of original construction, a series of seven interconnected locks (near Bezier), aqueducts that carry boats across rivers, a lock that allows boats to cross a river at grade, and a tunnel.*

> *With its complement, Le Canal de Garonne, the Canal du Midi operated as an important shipping channel till the mid-twentieth century. But as that century waned, so did commerce on the canal.*

In the summer of 1989 France suffered a drought so severe that stretches of the Canal were closed. This was the coup de grace to its Atlantic-to-Mediterranean commerce, and it became solely a pleasure-path.

That was the summer we decided to ride the ripples du Midi.

While a blue-smocked representative of the Blue Line explained the mechanics of the barge—speaking English, thank goodness, as

Belver's French was minimal—John, Carolyn, and I cased the craft. It had capacious staterooms and full heads fore and aft, a large lounge in between that made into another bedroom, and a roomy galley. The roof over the lounge slid back to let the air in. The boat was beginning to feel right. And the canal was now looking like a happy, burbly—if still tawny and narrow—body of water.

The Blue Line rep had just registered Belver captain-of-record when Kees, a Dutch information scientist and the last of our party, arrived. Kees ("case"), from Utrecht, had built his first sailboat when he was seven and had since navigated much of the world, often solo. He sailed regularly with Carolyn and Belver on the Chesapeake every summer. He would be our second captain. And his fluency instantly elevated him to position of main translator—although I had to repeat his French to the French, since his pronunciation was execrable.

We loaded our bags, food for breakfasts, and lots of wine for cocktail hours—including three shrink-wrapped bottles of plonk—and set off at full throttle—which is to say four knots, about 4 and a half miles an hour. The Great Captain was at the helm.

> The canal started off as a classic French allée, a path
> of water bordered by arches of plane trees. Many of the
> locks it flowed through were original, with gates of wood
> opened and closed by hand cranks. From time to time the
> canal shared its path with a small river, which doubled
> or tripled its width, and dirt berms gave way to low,
> grassy banks.

The first afternoon, we passed a couple of boats that were headed north, and we went through our first two locks—out of sixty-some more to come. Then five o'clock arrived.

> The canal is benign and forgiving for the most part; but
> it's totalitarian at the end of the day. At five p.m. the locks
> shut down and trap all vessels between their last lock and
> their next lock till seven or so the next morning.

I was certain we would starve some evenings as we wallowed in the interval between two locks with only wine and breakfast food at hand. But my fear was bootless. The first evening, after lock-in, we rounded a bend and discovered that someone's angel had thrown down a little village right there, including a good restaurant.

The next morning we opened the roof. The air was crisp. Through the plane trees, the sun dappled our breakfast baguettes and café au lait. The Great Captain cast anchor, and the easy current and puny engine drew Blueboy, as we called the boat, down the canal. We each settled down with books to wait out the drift toward the next lock. Kees kept an eye out for a small Asian woman, a girlfriend who said she might join us; and Belver kept a hand on the tiller.

We spent our time, as we did every day thereafter, entranced by the photo album of French life rolling by: the sheep farm and the farmer, the chateau and the well-heeled gentry, the vineyard and workers pruning the vines, the loom and the weaver, the small tin hut and the maker of wheelbarrows. We stopped now and then to buy local wine and, of course, to eat.

> *Most locks were simple rectangles. Deep ones, as much as two stories deep, needed walls that could withstand greater pressure, and were ovoid. Some held a single boat. Some could take two or three. Their gates ranged from ancient planks to simple rolled-iron sheets to modern reinforced metal doors. Most gates were operated by the lock-keeper— éclusier—who cranked them open. A handful had been automated.*

The locks that hadn't been automated became major sources of fun, as we could do much of the lock work ourselves—tossing ropes, tying up, cranking the gates open and closed. What with the locks, endless gazing at the landscape, peddling bikes along the footpath beside Blueboy, and various food-and-wine stops, our books went unread. Kees had brought along some 19th-century French erotica but, as he said, there was so much diversion that he didn't have time to turn on his pornograph. And somewhere en route he seemed to stop watching for his small Asian girlfriend.

> *Most locks were out in the country; a few cropped up in towns. Near Narbonne, the waterway became a small port, crowded with vessels of all sorts. In the middle of the congestion one had to find a handle hanging over the canal and tug it so as to open the lock gates.*

One late afternoon we docked beside a vineyard to replenish our wine supply. A large man met us at the door to the winery. He intuited that we were American and launched into a long spiel in rapid-fire French on Thomas Jefferson's visit to the vineyard in 1787. We gathered that Jefferson commanded a caravan of three barges, one of which was solely for wine, and he bought massive amounts of wine for Monticello. (Modern accounts would dispute the account; he seemed to be traveling lighter than that.)

We skirted several hamlets, a couple of large towns, and one village converted to a high-end refuge for English vacationers and ex-pats.

At lock-in time one afternoon, we put in at a village to use its post office and noticed posters advertising a circus that very evening. Indigenous culture and entertainment from locals turned us as giddy as five Margaret Meads in a midden heap in Samoa. We set up at a bistro table on the village square and had supper as the circus began setting up. There was a stage about one foot high with a curtain that looked like the tablecloths sold at farmer's markets, held up by aluminum poles stuck in the ground. Balloons of blue, white, and red were all around.

A five-piece band gathered. After a lengthy tuning-up period, the show began, and they started playing in such a way that you were pretty sure the tuning up was over. A few people in clown costumes came through the curtain and walked around, precipitating catcalls and whistles from the audience, that is, their friends and relatives. A young woman carried out a white longhaired cat. She sat it down and backed along the edge of the stage as the cat followed, its nose pressed to the tip of its mistress's index finger. There were cheers and applause. Next, a young man walked to the middle of the square with a brindle goat and said something that caused the goat to tap a fore hoof on the ground three times. The crowd exploded. We wandered off in search of less heady stuff.

The canal may be benign, but it did sometimes collude with the elements to play dirty tricks.

We believed that no peril could befall a slow plastic boat on a canal that was all but empty. But little perils did exist. The first: John was sunbathing on the roof alongside the bicycles; the Great Captain hadn't noticed some low-slung branches of plane trees till they swept bicycles and John off the roof and onto the deck.

Second: making a left turn under a bridge, Great Captain miscalculated and rammed the Blueboy's flank into a stone buttress, scraping the side of the boat, jarring our teeth, and jolting a medieval hamlet a few millimeters eastward. The second captain took over.

Et cetera: A couple of times, as we were sitting on the barge in the middle of a lock, changing levels, a light breeze on the starboard or port side was enough to blow Blueboy in a full circle—so underpowered he couldn't resist the slightest zephyr.

And so on: The last night of the cruise, we came into a wide stretch of canal—actually, a river—near a small village and started to tie up. A big blow—close to gale force—came up suddenly and started tossing Blueboy around like a cork. After a quarter-hour of naval orders shouted and whispered (did I mention that Belver spoke very softly and always issued critical orders into the wind?) and maritime clarifications, the two uber-experienced captains and three quite adequate crew finally got Blueboy tied down.

On the exhale, we noticed a sister barge nearby heaving violently as a young family of Brits on board tried to make for shore. The husband was at the helm, but the kids were too young to be helpful and the wife seemed confused. John and I leaped ashore from Blueboy, caught a line thrown by the husband, hauled them in, and trussed their barge to an oak tighter than a pig to a spit.

> *The locks were exciting but uneventful when they operated as designed. The locksman or lockswoman— éclusier or éclusiere—ushered your boat into the lock and closed the gates behind or in front of it. The water rushed in and raised your boat up, or rushed out and let your boat down.*

One late morning, we approached a pair of locks that would transport us down a steep hill. We were the fourth boat. The young éclusier loaded two boats into lock number one, and then a third— an elegant wooden barge half again as long as Blueboy—and let the water out. When the boats were down at the bottom of that lock, they had to wait for the water in lock number two to rise up to their level. Meanwhile, the gates behind them–old, like grey barn siding, and leaky—let a stream of water pour through a gap, gushing not into the bed of the lock, as it should have done, but into that last barge—right into its cockpit and down into the cabin.

The inhabitants—Swedes—began screaming and scrambling above- and below-decks as their barge began to sink. They located a large board and diverted additional water from their now half-sunk cockpit. A few minutes later, the fire company roared up, pumped out the water, and left.

And the éclusier went to lunch. At the open window of the charming yellow-and-red-ochre 17th-century éclusier's house he ate his government-sanctioned pro-labor lunch. Birds twittered, butterflies flittered, and the sun beamed sweetly on the waters, while forty or fifty people in waiting barges—now seven—seethed. In exactly one hour, the éclusier left his window and opened the gate to lock number two. The trapped boats moved on, and we eventually had our turn.

Our last day arrived. It was short, as we had to report to the dockyard in Montpelier by 1 p.m. The most unusual lock, one that crossed a river, lay ahead. The brilliance of this lock was that, as your boat approached, two sets of gates, one on either side of the river, swung open and shut off the river. Your boat would cross the river, the gates would close, and the river would flow once more.

As we approached, the shhh of water and hmmm of Blueboy's engine gave way to the bzzz of chain saws. A mighty wind the night before had sent branches and tree trunks into the machinery that operated the gates. The chain saws were trying to clear the machinery. So we cooled our heels while the hourglass was running out of sand.

Eventually the buzzing stopped, the gates swung open and held the river back, and we gunned the engine—if four knots could be considered gunning—and sped—if four knots could be considered speeding—to the finish line.

After ten miles or so, le Canal de Plaisir dumped us into a large lake and the marshes of the Camargue, where rice grows wild and little horses run free. On the far side of the lake, among the marshes, Blueboy found the miniscule opening that continued the canal and delivered us abruptly to downtown Montpelier, exactly on time. Our three cars were waiting, and we departed in unison, leaving behind a slightly scratched plastic barge, the two remaining shrink-wrapped bottles of rotgut, and a nonpareil week lazing through the French countryside.

20

The Bubble

Tackling the contradictions of Egypt
a couple of years before Tahir Square erupts.

We file into a stainless-steel tube. Cabin attendants lock the doors
and cross-check, triggering a chain of plane-airport-plane-airport-
plane-airport that transports us from one state of being to another.
In this case, from Philadelphia to Frankfurt to Cairo to Luxor—and
the lost millennia of Egypt.

It's 2009, two years before the Arab Spring.

* * *

Egypt never sparked my travel synapses—nor John's, I guess. Then
one spring day we sat on our back porch with two friends over a
salmon mousse. They were rhapsodizing about an upcoming Nile
cruise—a second honeymoon—and in a flash their visions of sailing
blue waters from one rare site to another on a luxury vessel began
to dance in our heads.

Even with its relatively peaceful profile in 2009, Egypt wasn't
a destination to choose offhandedly. Politics was in turmoil, as always, and safety couldn't be assumed: for instance, a young French
woman had recently been killed in the major Cairo market. For a
couple of aging Anglos with bad knees and no assault rifles, Egypt

was a precarious place.

But as our friends raved on, Egypt morphed into an alien, juicily forbidden mecca—maybe because we trusted our friends not to lead us into jeopardy. Barbara, who once cataloged books at the University of Pennsylvania, now danced folklorically (read: belly) under the nom de danse of Habiba, or Bibi. She and Ron (who had been a museum director, among other things) had traveled often and long to the Middle East—so much so that they'd been made honorary citizens of Tunisia (really). Bibi was in the process of interviewing a family of Egyptian dancers for an international belly-dancing magazine.

That evening, I e-mailed to say we'd love them no matter what their response, but would they mind if we joined them on their honeymoon? After a few days of silence—we didn't learn till mid-voyage that, unlike us, Ron and Bibi did not like to travel with others—they welcomed us aboard, we thought, warmly, but actually with trepidations about so much closeness.

* * *

The expectations that John and I harbored for the trip were half-baked. The fully-baked half included the certainty of sybaritic cruising on the glittering waters of the Nile, sipping tea on a pleasure boat under red-and-white-striped sails. The unbaked half included hazy visions of connecting with an ancient culture and experiencing the reality of Egypt as a living, breathing contemporary culture and a palpating geo-political entity—unbaked despite the fact that we had both read *Cairo: The City Victorious* (1998) in preparation. The author, Max Rodenbeck, lays out a compelling history and sociology of Cairo and Egypt from earliest times, chronicling its utmost glories to utmost seamy realities. John and I dismissed the seamy and built our expectations on the glory side.

Locked into the hurtling jet-powered silver bullet, we're locked as well into a vacation-induced bubble where we focus on our positive expectations and filter out everything else, and focus on our safety to the exclusion of unpleasant or dangerous realities. It's like being in a germ-free hermetic chamber for tourists.

After vibrating through 36 hours of fitful sleep, we land finally in Luxor, where darkness shrouds us in its own kind of bubble and a van shuttles us to a posh hotel, a former palace of King Farouk.

The next morning we wake in that privileged and protective wrap, and continue in another one that we deliberately contracted: a private van with hired guide and driver. They usher us through the City of the Luxor proper and across the Nile into the Valley of the Kings. Like every visitor, we are struck dumb by the almost art-deco architecture; heroic statuary of humans and animal gods and goddesses, and carvings reflecting ancient life, love, and high ceremony, still brilliantly colored after so preposterous a time; temples as vast as football fields sitting in even vaster sandstone plazas; gargantuan tombs of Tut and various Rameses. We are ankle deep in the dust of the primordial footprint of human history.

After three days, the owner of the cruise boat transfers Ron, Bibi, John, and me from our genteel hotel into his van and takes off toward Esna, where we will board. On the way, reality interrupts our merry progress: soldiers armed with assault rifles bring us to a halt and demand to know who we are and what our business is. The boat-owner/driver says he is taking these French tourists to his cruise boat, and the soldiers wave us through. (Americans would possibly have been detained or turned back.)

In Esna, we meet our 10 fellow-passengers-to-be at the suk (open market) and start wending our way toward the boat. Here, buffering the realities is impossible. The grime and debris of ages and fragments of modern trash is everywhere. People are dressed in rags. Children beg for "tips." Our travel group now appears to me like patrons of a human zoo, and our boat owner like a pimp who has trained the locals to perform tricks, such as turning a two-thousand-year-old spice grindstone on demand and handing around pita hot out of a stone oven. Instead of being amused, my conscience hurts.

But then we turn a corner and our false illusions bounce back. There is the Nile, with a couple of naked photogenic children splashing around and a woman photogenically washing clothes in the river. And our boat, the photogenic Meroe: all white, 171 feet long, 27 feet wide; lateen-rigged, red-and-white-striped furled sails hanging 45 degrees to the masts at each end. On the top deck, Venetian glass chandeliers hang under an off-white awning, above a hotel-lobby's worth of designer chairs, writing tables, and smartly upholstered banquettes, sofas, floor cushions, head cushions, and arm cushions.

As the boat begins to move, the guests—14 of us—settle onto one upholstered piece or another. Reedy shores start to unscroll on the left, desert cliffs on the right.

For five days, the crew pampers us with pillows, shawls, tea, and biscuits. The Nubian chef pampers us with moussaka, baked eggplant, salad with peas or carrots and cheese or tomato and parsley or just tomato, fava-bean falafel, braised beef, rice with vermicelli, fish tagine, fried chicken, fresh pita, fresh crepes and boat-made marmalade (breakfast), and coarse bread. One night he serves up sweet perch fresh out of the Nile. Stella beer and potable wine can be bought, and we bring our own gin for cocktail hour.

The boat itself pampers us with cushy quarters. Ron, Bibi, John, and I occupy the two staterooms, aft. They are all-white, like vanilla petit-fours inside-out, with large windows onto the purling wake of the boat and, sidelong, onto the distant shore.

Two or three times a day we passengers troop down the gangway into an excursion: a tiny temple carved into rock; a river-front farm walk with bananas and fava beans and donkeys and dogs; the massive temple at Edfu, with a relief of one of the Cleopatras; men in galabeyas—full-length, full-sleeved robes—loading cane from donkeys onto a barge.

Further upstream, the scale of time is terminally undone as we face the mud-brick fortifications of the 9,000-years-old El Kham settlement. If there had been significant rain at any point in those nine millennia, the bricks would have melted back into the earth.

It is also at El Kham that our bubble suffers further perforations. On the way back to the boat we pass through a tiny settlement, and our guide ushers a few of us into a home. The kitchen is an iron plate over a burner. Pigeons roost in niches in the sitting room. The sofa is stone, the floor is dirt. The children stand off to the side, beaming at us. One young boy wears a torn Nordic sweater. The kids look to be in need of a good dusting. I feel nervous at their attention; this time they are the patrons and we constitute the Zoo of Wealthy Tourists. I make a couple of faces at the youngest kids, and they laugh, and I feel better.

Their poverty—the lack of goods, absence of domestic technology like running water and electricity, the holes in the children's garments—doesn't surprise me. My grandparents, on their dirt-poor farm in southern Ohio, were just one click above it. But I'm surprised at the trash. Scattered around the bare, tan dirt of the complex are parts of plastic water bottles, worn-out car tires, and broken cardboard, all mixed into the dust.

Back in the security of the boat, we continue to the Kom Ombo temple, with its detailed carvings of the crocodile god, birthing apparati, and rampant spurting penises. The Nile is clear blue-green by this time, and some guests swim. After dark the crew build a bonfire on the beach, and drum and sing and belly dance (male format) around it. Bibi joins in with the female complement and becomes the happy star.

One day we take a four-hour trek along a wadi, an ancient trade route, to the top of the world, a stony peak, to watch the sun set over the rippled desert.

And all along the route are landscapes out of a book of clichés, the serene watercolors you wish you had painted: a spotted dog standing on the back of a water buffalo in green marshes, fishermen in tan galabeyas poling tiny skiffs, palm groves shimmering over pellucid waters.

The cruise ends in Aswan. It has been nothing but relaxed fun among John and me and Ron and Bibi. Their qualms have been banished and they claim they're ready for another trip with us. But they have business in Tunis and fly off from Aswan.

John and I fly to Cairo. The same guide as in Luxor, with a new driver, seal us into our private SUV. They tour us through the Great Pyramids, the Sphinx, the Sun Boat museum, temples, Coptic churches, the treasure-laden Egyptian Museum, and so on. Like the masses before us, we are gob-smacked by the creativity, beauty, and wealth Egypt contributed to the world through the ages.

But in and around Cairo, as well, the exotic falters and the shield for our delusions again falls away. Heaps of debris punctuate the streetways and stand beside the doors of seemingly prosperous homes. Canals are awash in plastic bottles and plastic wrappers from shore to shore. Alongside not-so-new roads are great heaps of aging construction detritus. Unfinished apartment buildings line the thoroughfares—red brick shells with frameless holes, waiting for windows till an apartment has actually been sold, and myriad buildings with concrete posts on top and rebar sticking out awaiting their last floors and a roof—all unfinished because buildings aren't fully taxed till they're completed. Large areas of Cairo are eternal construction zones, on hold, *sine die*.

Egypt and its womb, the Nile, have dwarfed us with beauty, dwarfed us with scale, dwarfed us with timeline, and affronted us with their audacity to muster at the dawn of history art so lustrous, thinking so deep, works so massive, human effort so focused and coordinated.

Do the rubble and rubbish result directly from Egypt's acute problems—under-regulation, corruption, over-population, under-GDP? Or are they metaphors for national desperation, for the grubbing life of the bulk of its populace, for its inability to pull itself up and out of its own social stink, for what Rodenbeck himself, referring to Cairo, calls its "shambolic grandeur and operatic despair"?

John and I load our mixed feelings onto a plane bound for Frankfurt and, eventually, Philadelphia. Our carry-on is the satisfaction of blending happily with Ron and Bibi on their honeymoon-renewal vacation and the indelible imprint of Egypt's antiquities, the beauty of its land, the enormity of its contributions to the world, and the very visible markers of its dysfunctions.

NESTINGS

21

Jousting in Landlordland

*A valiant try at owning 19 apartment units
and learning what never to do again.*

In 1974, the Stonewall riots of '69 were not yet considered a revolution, and same-sex marriage wasn't a hope to the most hopeful or a concept even to the most conceptual; so John and I wanted some cover for our new liaison. We were in Philadelphia, in our early thirties.

A house on Hazel Avenue provided a perfect subterfuge. Two rows of residences faced off across the street. Some were twins, some were in attached rows. But they were all Edwardian-style, all ochre brick set off with dentils and dadoes and Ionic columns. If a residence hadn't been remuddled—and ours hadn't—the inside echoed the Edwardian outside, with crown moldings, coffered ceilings, and chestnut woodwork. Cut-glass windows and doors threw rainbows around when the sun was right.

These amenities were compelling, but for us they paled against the layout. For camouflaging our relationship, the architecture of the house could hardly have been better. The first floor (living room, dining room, kitchen) would be the public floor; the second floor (a parlor and bedrooms) would be "John's"; and the third floor (more bedrooms), "Tom's." This is how we introduced the new house to friends and family. They were welcome to fabricate their own realities.

We bought it in the spring. A few months earlier, as winter was loosening its grip on 1974, we had begun the house hunt in the burbs, near John's apartment in Glen Riddle. Exercising the magnanimity that comes easily with young love, I agreed to forgo my city ways and entertain living way the hell out on the western frontier (suburbs).

On a Friday afternoon, an agent—face, name, gender I can't recall—led us to a house that backed up to a wooded ravine. It was plenty big—two floors, with entrances on both floors. By Saturday afternoon, we were poised to make an offer when the new work week began. However, the next day, Sunday, I woke up to the Kafkaesque notion that I had turned into a piece of dirty cheesecloth. On further thought, I gathered that the knotted-up, grey, porous, will-less feeling was depression and concluded that it came from the prospect of living in suburbia.

I came clean to John and recounted a premonitory moment of the day before: he had been wheeling us around our soon-to-be suburban countryside in his yellow Pontiac hardtop—amongst apple orchards, forested hills and vales, deforested tracts of expensive new houses, and small-scale manufactures in galvanized-tin sheds. We were at a stop light. I guess I was gazing at John with the blatant adoration of new love, complete with little red cartoon hearts pulsing out of my glistening orbs, when I noticed a young woman in the next car scowling at me as one might scowl at a mess of maggots. In my paranoia, I read that loathing look as the guarantor of homophobia in those faraway lands.

John agreed to house hunt in town.

I had been renting in Center City. But University City, right across the Schuylkill River, was not only more affordable, but was happily multi-ethnic, slowly gentrifying, tweedy, counter-cultural (flower children), and at least somewhat hospitable to gays.

We lit on Urban Developers and its realtors: Lois Bye, a slim sweetheart of a woman with a smoker's cough; and George Funderburg, large, irascible, unsmiling, intimidating, and Lois's husband. They personified University City for us: multi-racial, academic in tone and bearing, upwardly mobile with a social conscience, and former commune dwellers.

George and Lois showed us one and only one house—the one that was perfect, the one that we bought, the one we moved into: the twin in the 4600 block of Hazel Avenue, Philadelphia, US of A.

The house was perfect in ways other than looks and layout: it was in excellent condition. In the beginning, it needed nothing—tightening a drawer pull, pounding in a nail that had popped up on the stairs, patching a hole when we moved a picture. Our workshop consisted of hammer, pliers, screwdriver, putty knife, picture hooks, and spackling compound. We spent a lot of our weekend hours at the old Singer that John had inherited from his grandmother—perhaps because he showed a knack for sewing—making draperies for all the windows.

By the end of the first year, however, the perfect house began calling for attention and soon, drawing on my minor dabbles with carpentry and painting and John's more serious past with electrical and plumbing, we could savor the small victories of covering a ding in the wall, installing a dimmer switch, repairing a doorknob, hanging a bookshelf.

But escalation was rapid. In the second year we painted the outside of the house. Hiring it done was not in our budget at the time. What we knew to be a brick house with wood trim redefined itself, via its thirty-some windows and large wooden porches front and back, as wood-with-brick-trim.

Even though John and I always taught in the summer, the load was lighter than in the academic year; so we chose July, with its long daylight, to paint, after work and on weekends. John was acrophobic, so he worked on the lower parts. Tom was fool-hardy, so he tackled the upper—leaning out from a bouncy extension ladder, three stories over the sidewalk along the side of the house, to reach one Edwardian detail or another with a scraper or paint brush tied to a stick.

In the third year, 1977, drawing on what we had learned from our fathers and on hutzpah, we painted and papered a few rooms. We found fragments of an old chestnut cupboard set out for the trash and, with other fragments from in our basement, we recreated the original chestnut kitchen cupboard. Then the year got momentous.

Egged on by extra cash, free time, our successful DIY experiences and the lure of making a killing in real estate, we decided to become landlords. Our friend Don, from New Jersey, came along for the ride. His credentials were flimsier than ours: a school psychologist, a good cook, but not even our level of DIY chops. But he was willing to contribute dollar and sweat equity.

We went to George and Lois with our plan. They listened politely and said no: their mission was to sell houses for owner habitation, not for absentee landlordism or speculation.

But soon, Mike Something-or-Other, a realtor unencumbered by George and Lois's scruples, came along. Aside from stipulations in the deed (forbidding, for example, the manufacture of poudrette, a fertilizer made of night soil) and by the zoning commission (nix on a boarding house), he cared not a whit how we used a property. He sold us a house at the end of our block, just like our own, but long ago split up into six small apartments.

Becoming a landlord was that easy. And landlording went well. We confined our academic responsibilities to the campus, arriving early and staying late, seldom bringing work home. In the rare case when landlording demanded daytime, weekday attention, the flexibility of professorial duties allowed one of us to respond. Weekends we worked on upkeep on the apartments.

Overseeing the six units seemed doable and lucrative in the long haul, and four years later we struck again. Mike sold us a thirteen-unit building a few blocks away. In addition to manufacturing poudrette, the deed for that building forbade bone-boiling, which seemed to signal an iffier neighborhood than our own, and it was. We named the new building Squirrel Grove, and almost immediately Don found a decaying alphabet block in the back yard with an S on one side and a squirrel on the other. We took it as a good omen. We named the first building Nut Nest, as it was located on Hazel(nut) Avenue.

When Squirrel Grove came on board, Do-It-Yourselfism kicked in big time. Don would drive down from New Jersey early Saturday, and the three of us would work through the day, make a nice meal that evening, and work half of Sunday before Don went home. The to-do list was like the universe after the big bang: infinite and expanding: repair busted doors, refinish balustrades, install crown molding, sand and polyurethane floors, fix storm windows, replace outlets and switches, install light fixtures, remove old wallpaper, and paint, paint, paint.

We did our own plumbing, too, like changing faucets and spigots, and fixing toilets that ran. One Saturday afternoon, in the second-floor-front apartment in Nut Nest, John took a wrench to a valve on a leaky radiator. The valve broke, and the radiator erupted. Old Faithful, without the pauses.

Plumbing-supply stores had closed for the weekend, and no plumbing service could get there till Monday. Since the other apartments needed heat, we couldn't shut down the whole system, and for one and a half days, a small parade of passersby, feeding their basest schadenfreude, gawked as steam spewed out of the open joint and condensed on the windows and wallpaper peeled from the walls.

It was the end of plumbing for us.

Since Don lived a good hour away, John and I were the first responders to any problem with the apartments. It was *our* phone the tenants called. It was *we* who triaged the calls into immediate, next-weekend, maybe-later, and are-you-kidding categories. There were days when we didn't get calls, but not enough to remember.

Friday was always the worst. At 6:30 or so, John and I would come home from work with visions of Friday-night martinis, a roasted chicken, and a little Vivaldi. But the message machine would be flashing red with usually angry messages; "There's no hot water, again." "My air conditioner hasn't been working all day." "My key won't work in the outside lock." "My toilet won't flush." "There's water leaking into my living room ceiling." "There's water leaking from my toilet bowl." And so on. Note the frequency of water and toilets.

Some landlord responsibilities were predictable. When apartments turned over—which was frequently, given the transient nature of our tenant demographics (college students and marginally employed)—they had to be repainted, at a minimum, and often upgraded, like tiling a grotty bathroom floor, replacing an ugly ceiling light, or refinishing a floor.

Then there were the unpredictable, the Quixotic jousts in landlordland. One year, our plumber convinced us to replace the huge oil-fired water heater with individual electric ones, promising that we could charge a little more for rent to offset the installation and that the tenants, rather than we, would pay for hot water. But when we announced new rents, the tenants revolted, and we ended up eating the cost of the new heaters.

Every once in a while a tenant left owing rent, and by and by we ceased being surprised by it. They usually left in the dark of night, before we could follow through on our threats of eviction. One, however, didn't. He complained that the refrigerator was making too much noise. We replaced it with a silent model. He still refused to pay. Eventually the court ordered him to pay. Still he didn't; but at least he left.

Another year, a tenant moved out of Squirrel Grove and took the refrigerator (silent model) with her.

Four different roofers took three years to solve a leak in Nut Nest.

A Penn sophomore, living in Nut Nest, delivered what was

probably the coup de grace. Her snake had gotten out of its cage and disappeared into the wall. We failed to rise to the challenge, and I don't remember if she or Mommy or Daddy managed to retrieve the snake.

Things could have been worse. John and I both enjoyed our day jobs and got tenure. We became active in the neighborhood, participating in block parties, porch sales, and progressive dinners. We led the charge to replace the dying sycamores on the block and eventually became block captains. I became the block color-Nazi; at the kablang-kablang-kablang of a 54-foot ladder being extended, I was there with a paint chip of MAB Baltimore Cream.

And our own house was a joy. It hosted frequent dinner parties for six or ten and outdoor food fests for more; parties to celebrate the vernal equinox, the summer solstice, Bastille Day, and the Fourth of July. And Christmas parties, with two trees and a string quartet—Friday for gay and Saturday for straight, till we realized that the gay party was boring and merged them.

But one day we woke up to the fact that, outside the day job and the apartment buildings, our lives had became a null set. We were turning down invitations, forgetting social engagements, and losing more than a couple of friends. We were becoming resentful, too, at performing on someone else's schedule and taking care of spaces which, no matter how much time we spent in them, were not *our* space. Landlording had turned to drudging.

In the spring of '83 we put both rental buildings up for sale. In the darkest, dankest corner of the basement of Squirrel Grove we found two huge solid-walnut doors. We handed them over to an architectural salvage firm for three fresh hundred-dollar bills and blew exactly that on an evening for Don, John, and me at Le Bec Fin.

In the fall, John and I were vacationing in northern Maine; Don's school had started up, so he wasn't with us. Around noon on September 19 I put a lobster soufflé in the oven. A few minutes later, our lawyer called and cheered, "Congratulations. You're now ex-owners." He had taken both buildings to settlement.

The oven timer went off.

Out on the deck John popped the champagne.

A spike of steam from the soufflé reached straight up for the cloudless sky.

We saluted Cadillac Mountain across the glistering waters of Frenchman Bay and toasted goodbye forever to the landlord's life.

22

A Tail of Two Kitties

Two cats insinuate themselves into my allergic profile and change their humans' lives for years.

I grew up with dogs. First was Tippy, the black bird-dog mix with a touch of white on the end of his tail (tip-y), an obvious name coined by a child, like naming a fish Finny or a snake Wriggles. If he had been a more interesting dog, he might have been renamed Paintbrush or Tell-Tale as he grew up, but he was sort of ordinary—didn't do tricks or obey very well, barked at anything that moved—even large falling leaves—wasn't passionate about anything but escaping the house and the fenced-in yard. After Tippy was felled by a dose of rat poison, perhaps at the hands of an evil neighbor, he was replaced by a beagle-ish black and white pup who was quiet and sweet-tempered, and adored all members of the family. She was nicely proportioned as a pup, but her legs never grew much and she turned out squat. But her mature stature arrived too late; my brother and I had already named her after the leggy blond femme fatale on the Jimmy Durante show, Dagmar.

A canine sidebar in my life, spanning the Tippy years into the Dagmar years, was Jake, a true beagle and a hunting dog, who belonged to my grandparents, down on the farm. We saw him now and then, and the relationship remained superficial. Nevertheless, he counts as a dog.

If someone had asked, I could only have labeled myself a dog person.

My closest brushes with cats came in the form of trying to tame one or another of my grandparent's barn cats. But I could never break through their wildness, no matter how many chipped saucers of fresh cream I sat in front of them. Also, they were commodified, like all the other livestock. Every farm animal had a special assignment: pigs for pork, horses for plowing, cows for milk, cats for rodent control. When a superfluous litter was born under the house, Granddaddy put the kittens in a gunny sack with a couple of rocks and took them to the creek, as was the way, back then.

John and I moved in together in '74, into the Hazel Avenue house. He brought a dowry of an antique brass bedstead, a couple of bureaus, some family china, a yellow 1972 Pontiac sedan, and a tabby cat named Maude. I brought a beat-up American-built Sheraton-style sideboard that I had been keeping my underwear in.

When Maude was young, she lived with John in Michigan. She would walk along with him to neighborhood dinners and parties, and sometimes take a swim in the mill race. When she was a new mother, she lined up her mouse bounty on John's doorstep to show the kittens—three or four carcasses, all noses pointing in the same direction. She outwitted predative dogs. She came when called, as much as any dog. For three years in Tallahassee, she sat beside the typewriter as John toiled over his doctoral studies, and he dedicated his dissertation to Maude.

I bonded with Maude at first meeting. It probably took till the second meeting for her to bond back, being as she was a cat. She was a sleek, black-white-and-grey model, always ready for a good purr. If she wasn't getting enough love, she'd issue a moderated guttural roar that said "Better come over here and pet me, or one of us is going to be sorry."

When we were a few months into the new house, Mom and

Dad came up from Florida. They let themselves in while we were still at work and introduced themselves to Maude. They both—including Mom, who was an anti-felinist by genetics—were smitten. Even after I informed Mom that the lunch she had foraged from the refrigerator was the cat's all-vegetable dinner. ("I couldn't believe you would make such a bland dish.") Even after she caught Maude one evening sitting on one end of the leg of lamb, eating from the other.

Over the next two years I had time to assay Maude's qualities and found them to be of the finest kind. She was now eleven, and I concluded, sadly, that she didn't have much of a run in front of her. I suggested to John that we get a kitten so the redoubtable Maude could raise it in her image. John jumped at the idea. Happily, a friend had just bred her grey Maine coon girlcat (Abercrombie) and yellow tiger boycat (Fitch). A few months later, along came Chloé, a dirt-grey coon cat, with not a sign of tiger.

Chloé was introduced to Maude in the late spring. Maude hated her from the beginning and spent most of her waking time avoiding Chloé's clutches.

With the cooler weather of fall, we started keeping the windows closed, so the cat dander didn't get blown out of the house as thoroughly. That's when I started wheezing, weeping, sneezing and itching. The allergist said "You'll have to find the cats another home." I said, "I'll have to find myself another allergist," and did, and began a couple of decades of, first, weekly shots and, eventually, occasional inhalers.

Chloé was less predictable than Maude—even wifty. She would sit on a slug in the garden and carry it in on her withers, draw blood on my father's hand when he petted her too much, eat cicadas morning, noon, and night when they were in season, and scream bloody murder when we trimmed her nails. At one Christmas party, she waved her banner-like tail through a candle flame and caught it on fire. One evening she managed to catch a bat and get it into the house, where it scuttled behind a built-in bookcase that required demolition to extract. It was most certainly Chloé who was responsible for the Limoges lamp in the living room sitting upside-down on its shade, on the floor, one morning.

But she was dear, if scatter-brained. I was her mother substitute and she would hang onto my shoulder and purr for hours. She'd often settle on my pillow in the middle of the night and groom my hair.

Maude had her pure-cat moments—digging her way under the hot water heater on a winter's day; casting up hair balls on the Oriental rugs rather than on hard floors, carrying all my mother's embroidery skeins from the third floor to the first, one by one. But she existed largely on the human plane. She doted on human food (meats and vegetables) and loved parties (perching on my knee to absorb all the conversation). She was a noble cat.

In 1986, Susan Boynton, the cartoonist, wrote a book about two cats who were friends—cats named Chloé and Maude. I wrote her, saying that we had exactly two cats with exactly those names, and wasn't it a wonderful coincidence? She responded with a form letter.

Boynton's fictional Chloé and Maude were bosom buddies. We regretted that our cats would never achieve that state. Chloé wanted to play, Maude wanted to sleep. But as the years rolled on and our non-fictional Chloé and Maude mellowed, we would catch them snoozing in the same chair. They had achieved detente in sleep.

In 1986, we asked the surrealist Tucker Bobst to do a painting of Maude. It turned out to be an orange and black diptych, with a progression of solar eclipses and a sign of the Polish freedom campaign of the 80s, Solidarinosc on an op-art background. The next year we asked William Whiting, a trompe-l'oeil expert, for a painting of Chloé. It came in as a small primatif oil—Chloé sitting in a green-damask-upholstered chair with her right paw on a dead robin.

The next year Maude began sleeping most of the day as well as the night. She gently withdrew from the life of the house and became a shadow. In her few waking moments, she was feeble and woozy. We set up her food, litter, and bed in the den next to our bedroom; but she insisted on stumbling down to the litter box in the basement.

One Sunday a veterinarian friend made a call. I sat on the orange couch in the den with Maude in my lap and Jim administered the final injection. Her bladder emptied down my leg. We bawled like babies, and John came in and joined us.

Maude had a good run after she met Chloé: 12 years, for a total of 23, much longer than I had predicted. John thinks the tension between them contributed and claimed that Maude aspired to dance on Chloé's grave. But she missed the mark by nine years. Chloé lived on to 21.

Maude's ashes are buried in the back yard. Chloé's are closer: in the den, in a tin can, in a box, on the top bookshelf.

And I am a confirmed cat person.

23

Life Among Thespians

*Hosting a decade of actors
in our Philadelphia home-cum-inn.*

The Boys

Richard and Tucker scattered their lives over the northeast sector of the USA, including a good portion in Philadelphia. Theirs were lives of illusion and, like a double-throated siren, they drew us in.

Richard Maloy played the fat little rich boy in the second wave of the Our Gang comedies in early movies, and he traded on that his whole life. After baby fat gave way to handsome, solid maturity, he picked up acting parts when he could; wrote a few plays, a couple of which were staged through the kindness of friends; and, in his later years, worked on his memoirs. He was 150 percent Irish of which 100 percent was genetic and 50 percent feigned. He was verbose in what he imagined to be the Gaelic tradition; but the flush of his words more often confused than illuminated. No topic was too simple to be addressed directly: he spoke in sidebars and began his stories in the middle. In his theatrical moments (i.e., his waking hours) he affected Irish accents and speech patterns. "Ah, me dear," he might call down the table, "would you be passin' the ham?"

Like many people insecure in their positions, as he was in his place in the theater, he compensated by referring in name-dropping shorthand to things (theaters, plays) and, especially, people. For instance, he would blow "Irene" (eye-reenee), "Angela," or "Betsy" into the conversation like a spit ball, leaving you to pick it from your ear and puzzle out that it went with Worth or Lansbury or Palmer.

His preferred underwear was commando (none), and he was known to receive guests at home naked in warm weather. He could be as mischievous as a leprechaun.

(I've been unable to verify Richard's assertion of his Our Gang career in the many web lists of Our Gang personnel; perhaps it was too short a stint to be recorded. But standing one evening at a friend's toilet, I was confronted by an unmistakable Richard Maloy the child, imprinted in a photo of an Our Gang group imprinted on a decorative fan tchotchke.)

Richard's partner of many years was Tucker Bobst. He was heir to the wealth that financed NYU's Bobst Library, but an evil sister bilked him of his legacy because he was gay and left him with nary a sous. He was a painter. Whereas Richard's ism of illusion was impressionism through grease paint, Tucker's was surrealism through oils. He portrayed Baryshnikov against a background of theater tickets peeling off the front of Carnegie Hall with ostrich skeletons marching by; a tabby cat surrounded by the phases of the moon and the Polish uprising; a boy doing handstands horizontally, and trompe-l'oeil dollar bills on the stairs so real that people tried to pick them up. He punned frequently in his art, as when he depicted the tile walls of the Reading Terminal Farmers' Market riddled with bloody bullet holes and titled it *Cuisine Terminale*. He incorporated words in his art, undaunted by his inclination to misspell (Soladarinosc, trebel, fortenight). He sold paintings now and then, but they didn't command big prices. He often featured one of the rich and famous (president, movie star, etc.) in a painting and sent it off to the subject, gratis, for the promotional fallout. Tall and handsome, a jokester, an enthusiast for everything, with a laugh as rich as molten chocolate cake, Tucker was loved by everyone.

In the 1980s, when they were both in their late fifties or early sixties, Richard, who was a year older, legally adopted Tucker to secure visiting rights should one of them wind up in a hospital. Tucker, in his upper-crust Connecticut accent, began referring to Richard as "Fahthuh."

As starving artists, R and T, as they were known, bankrolled themselves through Tucker's art (again, not a princely income); through Richard's acting gigs, which were few, far between, and similarly unprincely; and through the rental of apartments in their house on 42nd Street. For large expenses and retirement they had built a nest egg—more robin's than eagle's—by buying one house after another, gussying it up, living in it for a while, and then flipping it.

The gussying up—which they had rehearsed scores of times before they arrived in Philadelphia—consisted of the yin of panache and the yang of impecunity. They favored flamboyant tableaux—heavy draperies and swags, artisanal furniture, large art, arresting tablescapes. Had they been well-off, they could have made grand statements easily, but without money they resorted to imagination. Renovation was mostly paint and wallpaper, and interior decoration leaned heavily on thrift shops and second-hand boutiques. Calling on their talents in on-stage and on-canvas illusion, they could turn a sow's ear of a place into an eye-catching silk purse. If you scratched its surface, you'd find a safety pin holding the back of a sofa cushion together; French hand-laid wallpaper terminating just below the top of the bureau; a large sculpture deflecting your eye from a 3-by-5-foot hole in the dining room wall; a shoji screen camouflaging a misplaced closet door. But the illusions worked.

On the Market

A few blocks away from their house on 42nd Street was our house, on Hazel Avenue. On a February day in 1985, the snowdrops out front were blooming, unusually early, and they turned our thoughts to not just warmer but calmer days.

That fall and winter had been dramatic. John and I had finally coughed up the cash to attend to long-deferred projects—reconnecting the gas fireplace in the second-floor parlor, rebricking the back patio, building another cupboard in the kitchen, and reroofing the house. All was good, till we got to the last project, the roof. An alcoholic contractor left the roof untarped, and a thunderstorm sent a torrent of water down all three floors and into the basement. In the months it took to dig out from the mess and repair the damage, all sense of joy in the improvements had evaporated and left us in a funk.

We needed some serious time away. While the snowdrops were giving way to the pink and yellow primrose of early spring, we plotted a September vacation across the Cote d'Azure into Italy and we felt better. When we cinched it with hard money down on hotel rooms, airline tickets, Eurail, and so on, we felt better yet.

Then, on an otherwise unremarkable April Saturday, came a phone call from the boys over on 42nd Street. "We've fallen in love with Annapolis yada yada decided to move yada yada putting the Bay house and this house on the market yada yada wonder if you'd be interested in one of them. Or both—ha ha," said Richard.

"The Bay house" was number 36 in Richard and Tucker's cavalcade of houses. It stood ten feet above the high-water mark of the Chesapeake Bay, protected by huge slabs of concrete rip-rap. The tan paint and crenellated roof line of the little house put you in mind of the Alamo; and that was its name. Par for their standard business plan, R and T had found it a ruin and left it a charming vacation house with a good profit margin.

"This house" was house number 35, their home on 42nd Street, a semi-detached affair built at the end of the Civil War for the widowed daughter of a Philadelphia financier. Touted as "a Second-Empire Italianate Villa" when it was new, it gave up its role of villa when it got parsed into six apartments, probably in the 1940s. Richard and Tucker lived in the largest and rented out the rest, fully furnished.

The following Tuesday—shot through with 1) anxiety over possibly losing our Grand Franco-Italian Vacation, 2) the would-be irony of abandoning the brand-new expensive renovations at Hazel Avenue, 3) the self-inflicted irony of becoming landlords again only two years after unloading 19 emotionally painful apartment units, and 4) excitement over a new home and an inn-keeping adventure on 42nd Street— we returned their call.

"Let's talk about 42nd Street," we said.

The Sell

John and I were 43 and 45 years old. We had known Richard and Tucker—older than we by 13 or 14 years—for several years and had been in each other's homes numerous times for meals or parties. But we had never gotten beyond their first floor and didn't know even broad-brush particulars of their rental business, except that the apartments were fully furnished and that actors occupied them during the theater season. When John and I sat down with them, it was a seminar, and they were the teachers.

Years earlier (number uncertain, as per many of Richard's "clarifications"), Richard had developed a connection with the Philadelphia Drama Guild. The Drama Guild was a regional theater company, meaning that a director and actors were assembled from scratch to perform a particular play. Sets would be built, lighting designed, and costumes rented or made. The director and actors rehearsed for four weeks and performed for three, then disbanded forever.

Richard snagged a bit part with the Drama Guild here and there. By and by, his connection led to a contract to house the actors and directors—up to five, one in each apartment, for seven weeks—times five, for the season's five productions. It was guaranteed income, and that was a boon for the perennially cash-strapped R and T.

"Will the Drama Guild contract continue with new owners?" we asked.

"Yes."

"Would we have enough time to keep up with it?" we worried. "We do have full-time jobs, you know."

"Piece of cake. You turn over all apartments at once, on Sunday, five times during the season."

We fretted that we would be indenturing ourselves to calling cabs, ironing frocks, feeding lines or peeled grapes—whatever these divas and divos could think up. "Ha ha. No. They're not like that at all."

John and I looked at each other. OK, ask the next question, our eyes said.

"So what are you asking?" I ventured.

"$25K for the furnishings of the rental apartments, except the sectional daybed in 2F, plus $225K for the building and grounds," said they. A quarter of a million. In 1985 dollars. Holy shit.

Playing himself like an organ, Richard pulled out all his dramatic stops to convince us, first, that we had a real bargain on our hands; second, that several competitors were ready to pounce on the bargain; and third, that with our salaries at Drexel we should have no problem meeting the mortgage payments. (He had cannily estimated our combined annual incomes within plus-or-minus 2%.)

Our lawyer prepared a counter-offer. I don't remember the amount, but as we sat in the second-floor parlor of 42d Street five days later, Richard, in stentorian baritone, intoned, "This is insulting." Tucker giggled nervously. Not only were they affronted by the price but, judging by their sounds of scorn (fah...pooh...fuh) the "broom-clean basement" codicil was sticking in their throats like a spoonful of mouse gleet from the basement floor. And our use of a lawyer was just as odious. "In our [gazillion] real estate deals over [gazillion] years," boomed Richard, "we have *never* used a lawyer."

Threatened by purchase competition (a damned lie) and romanced by the running of a house of theater folk, with undertones of being had, we buckled two days later—agreed to their price, on their terms. Richard offered to toss in an antique English cupboard in their dining room for a modest price, which we accepted, and that sectional daybed (grungy), which we astounded him by refusing.

A contract was born, and settlement was scheduled for September.

The Move

We annulled the Cote d'Azure vacation and got what refunds we could, put the Hazel Avenue house up for sale, and started packing immediately.

Spring took off like a shot toward the settlement date, giving us barely time to fill to pull things together for the movers. As I was committed to four weeks of consulting in Memphis that summer, John bore the brunt of the packing.

At 7 a.m. on September 19th, the largest truck in the North American Van Lines fleet drew up, with a smaller one in its wake. By 1 a.m. the next morning all our possessions, even the firewood, had been set in their rightful places at our new home.

Two days later, we threw a small dinner party to christen hearth and home as only shared food and drink can do.

The day after that, five new tenants moved in.

And the day after that our new term began at Drexel.

Keepers of Thespians

Forty-second Street was a turnkey operation. Each apartment had the necessary furniture, and clean sheets and towels were ready and waiting in the faux-wood-painted linen cupboard on the third floor. We needed only to clean the apartments, make the beds, and supply their first breakfast. No sweat, we thought, and no sweat it was.

As the first five actors trickled in late Sunday afternoon, we greeted them in awe. Didn't know who they were, and didn't care. Their mere association with the stage was enough to fog our minds.

Later we learned that we wouldn't recognize most of the actors' names—OK, so Lou Rawls's sister was in the first batch—because big-name actors weren't signing up for regional theater anymore. Richard and Tucker had housed Angela Lansbury, Irene Worth, Betsy Palmer, Chita Rivera, Bernadette Peters, Claire Bloom, Sir John Gielgud, and other luminaries. By the time we arrived on the scene, stars of that ilk had larger fish to fry than rehearsing a part they may never have done before, or might never do again, for a short run and not a lot of gelt or glory.

Nonetheless, we housed a few stars over the years: Robert Sean Leonard (*Dead Poets' Society*), Tovah Feldshuh (a friend had to draw our attention to her fame), Julie Hagerty (*Airplane*), and Julia Meade (who once sold Lincoln Town Cars on the Ed Sullivan show). Campbell Scott, offspring of George C. Scott and Colleen Dewhurst, passed through and left behind some Jockey briefs that I wore for years. Being far from star-struck, we may have unwittingly housed a few other biggies. Nonetheless, most guests were journeyman actors—talented, but not celestial.

But when that first corps arrived, stars or not—shazam!—we were theater people. We snorted the rarified perfume of the strutting life and glimpsed the mask and mystery of dissimulation and were won over, no further ado. The Drama Guild immediately adopted us. We attended every opening-night performance, every celebratory party, dinners at the managing director's home, and all DG special events. For our part, we hosted dinners for every corps and, in the summer, cook-outs for the DG staff.

Far from being spoiled brats, the actors were well within the range of regular folk. They worked hard: four weeks running lines and rehearsing and then eight productions a week for three weeks. They proved to be considerate, kind, and surprisingly normal personalities with an edge of quick and clever. And appreciative: they had all experienced accommodations from hell (abandoned motels or a fraternity house vacated for the summer; double- or triple-bunking; no phones; and worse). So they loved our clean, fully equipped, private-phoned, single-occupant apartments. They brought us presents, sometimes, and at the big dinners, they filled the house with the rattle of jokes, drama, comedy, a recited poem, ribaldry, and high wit—as close to a salon as we'll ever get.

But even under our theatrical rainbow, the realities of house and neighborhood had to be tended to.

One was crime. When we moved into 42nd Street, crime was rampant. Most of it was petty, but rape and murder occurred, too, though rarely. We were without a hint of how to prepare for big violence, except to install an alarm system and keep my grandfather's Masonic sword under the bed. About the petty stuff, we learned to never set out flowering plants before the end of May, for that's when the smart juvenile delinquent shops back yards for Mother's Day; never leave a chair or table, no matter how cheap or rickety, on the front porch overnight; never leave anything visible in the car overnight, even a bag of kitty litter; and never leave anything (pipe cutter, table saw, box of plumbing tools) unsecured even for two minutes, even in broad daylight.

Still, shit happened. A one-armed bandit (really) made the rounds of the neighborhood for a while—once, poised on a ladder, ready to squeeze through our bathroom window; another time, dragging an actor's purse, under her horrified gaze, out the first-floor-front window with his artificial limb.

Another cat burglar cut the screen on the second-floor-rear apartment and made off with the pants-with-wallet of another actor (David Schramm, who played Roy on the TV sitcom *Wings*).

Gradually—and I don't know why—the cat burglars declined in number and in quality. One summer noon, about the same period the *Philadelphia Inquirer* was reporting that even smart electric typewriters had been outdated by the personal computer-plus-printer, our next burglar fell off our back porch roof into John's rhubarb plant trying to make off with a 20-year-old manual Remington of street value zero. Our last cutpurse was carrying off a neighbor-lady's microwave when neighbor-lady nailed him with a can of Campbell's tomato soup pitched like a hardball to the middle of his back, and he fled.

Crime subsided, in time, and our anxiety for the wellbeing of the thespians and ourselves relaxed.

In the meantime, the house retained its urgency. Restoring and maintaining a building so complex that its roofs could be described six ways (mansard, flat, pitched, asphalt, slate, rubber) kept us more than entertained. With its potential for elegance and an innately Victorian cachet, the house demanded deep cosmetic *make-up*. Every evening and weekend for five years we patched holes, sanded and polyurethaned floors, painted or papered every room and closet, retiled bathrooms, sewed draperies. And so on. The grand house came under our control as much as such a compound edifice can. Cosmetic *surgery*, like wall-moving, kitchen-gutting, or bathroom-rebuilding, waited for later years.

Outside, we removed three layers of fencing around a dog run in the back yard and unearthed a full Big Wheels and wheelbarrow loads of other detritus. We replaced many square yards of ivy and weeds with proper borders, removed a long-dead horse-chestnut tree from the front yard, and tamed the wisteria that had been growing with minimal discipline on the front veranda for over a hundred years. The gardens matured and won an award or two.

And our professor careers were going swimmingly, with tenure, advancement in rank, consulting gigs, publications, and administrative responsibilities.

Our lives were good, and the theater connection made them better. The legacy from Richard and Tucker, the Drama Guild, perfused our days from September to May. They brought us the paired faces of Janus, comedy and tragedy, and the paired gifts of content and process—of the creative mind laid down on the dramatic page and of life's adventures in capturing character and moment. As they sat at our table or stood talking in our halls or performed (personally, just for us, of course) they wove themselves through our social fabric, snagged our hearts, and furnished our minds.

For ten years, the theater intervention made our otherwise full and happy lives fuller and happier. When the Guild went belly up, bankrupt, in 1996, it left a hole in the villa on 42d Street, and in us, that spackle or peat moss couldn't repair. We had no choice but to settle for the old comfort of our former lives, washed with the residue of the joyous thespian occupation.

24

Raising the Phoenix

*In the dead of night, eleven humans and two cats
find the living room in flames.*

Commotion upstairs, seeping into the basement where we're sleeping: faint footsteps overhead in the hall, rustling around in the kitchen, muted urgent voices. Then hollers burst down the stairs into our deep sleep: "Tom, John!"

It was the middle of the night, and we had a full house. The five rented apartments were occupied one actor in each; and in our own apartment there were more than just John and me. Our friend Arthur had arrived the afternoon before with a couple of friends: a younger woman named Mits (or Retz, or something that ended with a ts sound), and an older one named Jess, both in Birkenstocks and carrying little except their yoga mats. We gave up our bedroom on the first floor to the women; Arthur crashed on the orange corduroy Hide-a-Bed in the den; and John and I and the two cats retired to the trundle bed in John's study, in the basement.

"Tom, John! C'mere!" Faint from lack of sleep and perhaps a little too much "medicine" at dinner, John and I clamber up into the kitchen, where our guests are bellowing that the house is on fire. We panic, of course, but our cobwebbed brains lead us into rote, but untested, responses, as we stagger frenetically into several nooks to locate the fire extinguisher, yell for everyone to get the hell out of the house, yell for each other to call 911, wonder if all this is really happening, and guess how big is the fire and how much time we have to get out.

Meanwhile, someone of sounder mind has already called 911 and, before we can get all the humans and cats out of the house, screaming sirens and strobing red lights are at the curb. The ten of us, bath-robed or street-clothed, file out into the night. It is October and blessedly mild. We stand there, in fire-colored light strobing from fire-colored trucks, as nearby residents gather to witness as much catastrophe as they can. John and I are numb with disbelief, but with enough feeling to be embarrassed by all the public attention to what had to have been our stupidity or the stupidity of the electrical system or whatever caused the fire. The sirens whimper down to silence and the firemen begin their work. John and I hand the cats back and forth to keep them from spooking and running away.

It soon becomes clear that no one is in danger and the fire is contained to one room, and everyone seems to relax. Still, firemen take no prisoners; nothing stands in their way of conquering a fire. They stride down the front hallway, dragging a fire hose. I follow to see what I can. They break through the living room door—whether by foot, shoulder, or axe, I don't remember. Two sofas, the only furniture in the room, are burning; the floor is on fire; at least one can of paint is flaming. At that point I am told to leave the house. The fire jockeys hose down the flames and eventually heave the smoldering sofas through the living room windows—without pausing to open them—and into our ancient azalea hedge.

After inspecting ground zero and surrounding rooms several times, the ranking fireman declares the fire extinguished and the house safe. There is surprisingly little fire-stink outside the living room. John and Arthur and I secure its damaged door and cover the gaping window holes with four-by-eight plywood panels that were waiting in the basement for another project. With collective exhalations, we go to our respective beds. The cats pretend nothing has happened. John and I are surprisingly soon asleep. I may or may not have relived the night's commotion; but I certainly dream of the work that lies ahead.

It was 1987, and redoing the living room was our big project of the year. We had owned the house for 18 months. It had six apartments, five of which we rented out to actors for local productions, and one of which we lived in. Like an aging starlet, the house needed deep cosmetic work. Fortunately, John and I had learned from our fathers—painting and a bit of carpentry from my dad, electricity and plumbing from John's. And we had a friend or two who were handy and eager to help. We had tackled the dining room first, and turned it into a fantasia of Victorian décor: below the picture rail, embossed paper stained to look like leather; above it, French hand-laid wallpaper that looked like tapestry; crimson draperies and swags and portieres festooned with elaborate fringe; an antique Queen-Anne-style wooden grill; and friezes at the ceiling that we had bronzed when a friend suggested sarcastically that we might as well gild the lily.

Now, a year later, we were putting the finishing touches on the living room. It wasn't going to be over-the-top Victorian—more of an English gentleman's lounge. We had stripped off the old wallpaper and painted the walls parchment and the ceiling the medium blue common to French shutters. I had gold-leafed a scattering of stars on the four corners of the ceiling. Our friend Bill had tromp-l'oeiled the two-foot-high frieze around the room to look like tan-and-grey marble. He had finished it just yesterday.

The last step in the living room renovation was to resuscitate the fireplace surround. It was oak, and it had sustained enough grime and smoke in 122 years to turn its swarthy Jacobean stain nearly black.

I whomped up a potion of equal parts turpentine, vinegar, and boiled linseed oil—a mixture that we had come across years ago and had often used to revive dull and darkened woodwork in Squirrel Grove. We called it the Magic Mixture.

But we were ignorant, to our everlasting regret, of its perils.

After John wiped down the surround with old terry rags wet with the Magic Mixture, its grain showed, and it glowed with new life. The room was now officially finished. The next day, with the help of our visiting friends, we would move its furnishing out of the dining room into the living room. But tonight, too exhausted to do more, John stuffed the used rags in a plastic trash bag and left it beside the two large beige sofas, the only furniture in the room. Our footsteps echoed out of the room, and we closed the door.

In the wee, dark hours, the rags spontaneously flickered to life. Flames engulfed the bag of rags, set fire to the floor beneath, and spread to the sofas. Cans of paint exploded and burned. The Magic Mixture became a torch.

A few actors, returning in the early morning from post-production eating and drinking, opened the door into the front hallway and saw dark smoke puffing out of the crevices of our living room door. They broke through the door next to it, into our dining room, and alerted everyone in our apartment and in the other apartments. It was one of those folks who called 911.

The day after the fire, we continued to play host to our personal guests in the undamaged part of our apartment, till they departed for their respective homes. But not far under the surface of our hospitable presences, we were calculating how to fast-stream the resurrection of the living room and upper apartments.

Within a few days, the insurance adjustor came calling, and an agreement was reached on the spot. A couple of days later a check was issued. Smoother than expected. Restoration could now commence.

When the firemen crashed through the living room door, the blackened smoke and soot inside roared up the stairs and settled into all the fabrics on the second and third floors. Every piece of clothing and drapery on those floors went to the cleaners, and professionals were brought in to wipe down the upholstered furniture. At ground zero, the living room, every surface was professionally cleaned. What that gained us was not presentable surfaces, but surfaces ready to do all over again—gilt stars, marbleized frieze, and all.

As for rebuilding, someone—to his or her salvation, we don't remember who—referred us to a "contractor" for the restorations, a man who had taught industrial arts in a local high school and had recently started a "construction firm" that consisted of just him. With no alternatives to consider, we hired him, and from the beginning he proved to be an unfaltering amateur. Every facet of his work—woodworking, tongue-in-groove flooring, window installation, even painting—required correction on top of correction. Some of his errors, like the repair of the flooring, was done so ineptly it couldn't be fixed without a major demolition and re-do—which we didn't have the funds for. We bore with his blundering efforts till the room was as good as he was going to make it and gave him the final check to get him out of our hair.

Our friend Bill was not happy when we asked him to come back and redo his marbleizing work. His kind of creativity abhors covering the same territory twice, and he grumbled the whole time. We haven't seen him a lot since. But when he had made it just as it was before, the room had finally risen like a phoenix from its ashes and soot. Even before the replacement sofas arrived, it showed off the other furniture, art work, draperies, lamps, and tchotchkes as planned. The tall oak fireplace surround—unscathed by the conflagration—gleamed sarcastically.

And John and I phoenixed with the room, in two ways: we restarted, immediately, to invest another quantum of energy in doing what we had already done, somehow setting aside the bitter ashes of a ruined effort and getting back to work. And, maybe as a consequence, we were able to rise up and leave behind—quickly and completely, as far as I can tell—the panic of that night of the fire and to return to nights of calm sleep.

25

Lower, Slower

*Small-town and big-city contrasts
turn from accidental to deliberate as we bi-habitate
in Philadelphia and Rehoboth Beach.*

Every place we visited, if we liked it, we toyed with buying a second home. On our second trip anywhere, John would start lingering in front of real estate offices, studying the house-for-sale adverts. We knew full well that in places like Avignon, Barcelona, Paris, and London home-owning was beyond our means. In the relatively near reaches of the US, where prices could be more modest, we had long since indulged in serious daydreaming with a few close friends about building a vacation compound in Down-East Maine and just between John and me about buying a summer place in Province-town, Massachusetts. But the daydreams were dampened by the demands of owning a place seven or ten hours away—retaining a caretaker, managing repairs from a distance, and driving seven or ten hours in case of an emergency—and we never followed through.

In the early '90s, we started visiting our friends Bill and Rob-ert in their succession of waterfront homes near the beaches of southern Delaware. The string of Delaware beaches—Rehoboth Beach, Lewes, Dewey Beach, Bethany Beach—constituted a calm

resort, unlike the rowdy shore of New Jersey. In fact, life throughout the state's southernmost, third county, Sussex, was relaxed.
It was known and is known still as Lower, Slower Delaware (LSD
on bumper stickers), a land where the citizens, especially those in
the construction and maintenance trades, weren't compelled to do
something today if they could put it off till tomorrow. LSD the drug
is not necessary.

By the end of our second trip to Bill and Robert's, real estate
brochures began peeking out of John's back pocket and his side of
the mattress, especially ones touting Rehoboth Beach.

Bill and I had been friends since 1942, when we were two years
old and lived next door to each other. As we grew older and moved
apart, the mucilage of our mothers' correspondence held us together enough that we were able to reconnect in our thirties. By
the mid-90s, Bill had retired and was writing blurbs for those very
real-estate dreadfuls that John was poring over on the not-so-sly.

After three or four weekends in Lower, Slower, since we liked
the ocean airs, the small town environment, the restaurants and
bars, and the gayer-than-average population, John began proposing
that we "just see what's out there." It would have been the first anyone in our families had extended themselves to a second home, and
the idea felt like an extravagance.

But in a few more trips, the proposal started sounding reasonable to me and perhaps even partially my idea. Bill pointed us to Realtor Sharon and for two years, every time we were in the area, Realtor Sharon engaged us in a search. She showed us places all over the
countryside, but consistently outside the town centers and further
from the ocean, where prices were more attuned to our budget. After numerous weekends of interesting but fruitless searching, we
realized that these houses were so far from the tourist centers—the
ocean—that they would have to be rented for the whole year, rather
than week-by-week, and that, therefore, we couldn't use them even
for an off-season weekend.

We were about to throw in the towel, when Bill mentioned a

house he had just blurbed. It was in downtown Rehoboth, not out in the country. "We might as well drive by," he said.

It backed up to a tree-lined street and, across another street, faced a lake: a white-stucco beach cottage. "Cottage," in the sense of being a vacation house, can range from a one-room log cabin in West Virginia to a golden age mansion in Newport, Rhode Island. This was somewhere in between. Bill called the broker. In two minutes a black Mercedes squealed up, and Realtor Debbie popped out in full effervescence: smiling, laughing, bubbling. She let us in the back door and raced ahead to turn on lights and raise the shades to let in the view.

Before we entered the gauntlet of buying another home, I knew that the idea of "home" is a beast of many dimensions and countless variables—from interior aesthetic (comfort zone or House-and-Garden fantasy or easy-care abode) to exterior aesthetic (treed, meadowed, on water, in a desert, secluded, and so on) to demands on personal time (fixer-upper, move-in ready), to economic (investment, estate-building, a necessary expenditure for shelter).

This list isn't even close to exhausting the variables, but John and I had agreed before we started looking in southern Delaware that investment was our sole driver. Rent it out for the summer months, maintain it during off-season weekends trips down from Philadelphia when the University didn't have a call on our time. It wouldn't be a bad place to stash some idle cash and dip our toes in the real-estate waters of southern Delaware.

We also agreed that we wanted to spend some time in that second home, and we knew ourselves well enough to admit without saying that interior and exterior aesthetics—not just rentability—would play a major role in winnowing through candidate houses.

Following Realtor Debbie, I walked through, in total-investment mode. Well, maybe with a sub-mode of self-centered aesthetics. The first floor had pretty high ceilings. The kitchen, where we entered, had ample counter space and new appliances, including boiling water on tap. What's more, it looked through the dining room, out the French doors, across the screened porch, and onto Silver Lake. Wow. Quite rentable. Two living rooms and a long screened porch all opened one into the other. I eventually counted six bedrooms and four baths. I could see the lake from all the public rooms and four of the bedrooms. From the deck on the second floor I could see the ocean. And the private dock. Pretty darned rentable. A two-block stroll to the ocean: *very* rentable.

The place was offered fully furnished, at no extra charge. The furnishings weren't high end—hard materials of wicker, faux wicker, and rattan; soft materials dated at least twenty years by hues of mauve, pink, and periwinkle—the draperies, too. But they were functional and in good condition. Pearl-grey walls throughout. Livable.

And rentable. And move-in ready.

Back in the kitchen, tour over, John and I locked eyes. His were glinting with more than the lust of investment. They were saying, "nest, nest, nest." Silly me. Debbie smiled and laughed her lyric-soprano laugh and said, "I'd like to sell you this house."

That afternoon John and I ran the figures. The price was double our budget. On the other hand, we estimated that 12 weeks of summer rentals would cover mortgage, taxes, and utilities if we put 50 percent down.

Later, we sat at a small dinner party at Bill and Robert's. In the course of small talk, we blurted out our encounter with the house to two of their friends, Bonnie and Linda, transplants from Pittsburgh. Their reflex, "Buy it!" was so forceful that it almost sounded greedy, as if they wanted to suck us in to either share the misery or contribute to the tax base. They asked when we were going to retire. "No intention," said we, truthfully—although we were inching close to retireability, financially. Through smirky smiles they wagered that, first, we'd find more and more reasons to drive down to the house and, second, we would retire as soon as we could.

The next morning, Sunday, when we should have been out having a nice brunch, Realtor Debbie showed us through the house again, and we talked price. John and I called our respective fathers in Gainesville, Florida and Kutztown, Pennsylvania—who were also forgoing Sunday brunch—and wangled advances on our inheritances. We tagged certain of our stocks and bonds for liquidation. By dinner time, we had a signed agreement of sale.

We settled on the house in September and visited it frequently through the winter, making it ready for renters and, to a small extent, coherent with our style of living. By June, rentals started, duly honoring our investment motive.

But the domestic imperative had already kicked in, almost the minute we signed the purchase agreement. Neither of us could stave it off. Starting with the repellant colors in the living room draperies—replaced even before the first renters turned the doorknob—our need to declare the place aesthetically ours spread like a Santa Ana wildfire to sofas, chairs, tables, beds, lamps, and rugs. Within three years there were few of the original furnishings left. and we had faux-finished every wall on the first floor with pigments we brought back from France.

And, as Bonnie and Linda promised, we found more and more reasons to make the trip to Rehoboth. No, "reason" is not the word; it had little to do with ratiocination or practical requirements. "Passion" is the word. We were besotted with the place and driven to hang out there as much as possible.

Water was certainly a key to our passion. Growing up in mostly land-locked Ohio—John in Bowling Green, me in Chillicothe—where the only lakes other than distant Lake Erie are man-made and few, water-gazing had a mystical, undeniable allure. Now to own a place close to natural bodies of water—a bona-fide lake and an actual goddamn ocean—was almost too idyllic to be real. Eight years later, as we sat on the dock, martinis in hand, sun setting on our backs, water lapping at the pilings, these two boys from Ohio were still pinching themselves out of their elation at having come down in this great good place.

It took longer to realize that a major attraction of Rehoboth came from scale—from its size, compared to the metropolis of Philadelphia.

John grew up through his baccalaureate years in the flats of northwestern Ohio, where everyone knew everyone else and watched out for each other. I grew up through high school primarily in the hills of south-central Ohio, where our house backed up on an asparagus farmette, where you could walk across town in an hour, and where the elementary school, the junior-high, the high school, the drug store, and the five-and-ten, were ten minutes from home, by foot.

Then John and I ended up in a big city—Philadelphia. We got used to theater and musical theater, drama, opera, world-class orchestra and museums, good restaurants, and a variety of other entertainments; the historicity of colonial buildings and gardens; the demographics of diversity; the rich, vibrant urban life. We became accustomed to being far removed from the workings of local government and to big-city anonymity, the comfort of being a stranger to almost everyone, not being accountable all the time. We also got used to the egregious effrontery of many municipal employees, the goodness of whose days are directly correlated with the badness they can induce in yours—the trouble they can visit on you in filling out a form or finding an office in City Hall or locating a deed.

In Lower, Slower we realized that, more than hankering for a water feature or a home in a resort town or a home in a *gay* resort town, scale fueled our passion: a small town, a village, really, where the Licenses Office consists of Judy and only Judy; where city workers sometimes do the special thing, like pick up a bag of trash when it's not the right day; where you run into someone you know everywhere you go; where back-fence conversation is the primary social medium. Where you're close to government and able to reason with it, and incompetence in municipal employees happens usually from innocence rather than blockheaded intransigence. Where you're more noticed, more accountable, more vulnerable, and, ultimately, we hope, more cared about—more like the places we grew up.

Footnote: Today, Rehoboth Beach is more Big City than it was back then—more bureaucracy, less transparency, more aggravation, and so on. But still feeling like a small town that, by and large, cares.

26

Possessed

The joy! The guilt!
Burdened down and buoyed up by stuff.

Getting Things

Our first house is a ten-room twin on Hazel Avenue in West Philadelphia. The notary has hardly pressed her seal into the deed when possessions start rolling in—largely through John—stuff that had been awaiting liberation from his family's garages and basements: grandmother's Victorian walnut bureau; grandfather's honey-oak bureau with graceful legs and graceless body; a huge walnut drop-leaf dining table with a leg every place you want to set a chair; over 100 pieces of Great Aunt Helen's Spode dinner service; a stack of oriental rugs; five rush-seated pine chairs; an antique glass canister set with tin lids; and so on. You get the drift: big and small, and mostly old, with the patina of age, many of them pleasing. Not too shabby a haul.

My contributions are measly: A Sheraton sideboard that had been left behind in my first Philadelphia apartment, where I kept my underwear and T-shirts, a tall chest of drawers from a thrift shop, an antique honey-oak pedestal dining table, and five Italian chrome-and-plastic dining chairs from Wanamaker's.

John comes to acquiring naturally. His mother loved to shop and had an eye for quality, and she passed those traits on to John. He grew up with nice things around him. I, by contrast, grew up more modestly, with objects necessary for survival: bed, sofa, kitchen table, and so on. Mom applied an eye to style and design to the extent the dollar allowed, but it was function, not form, that ruled our acquisitions. And budget wasn't the only governor on our buying machine; Dad's career with the United States Bureau of Prisons subjected our family to moving anywhere in the country with as little as a week's notice, from one furnished government-owned house to another. Living on the light side of the possessions ledger made sense, and I grew to regard it as the right and moral path. You owned what you used, and not much else.

Getting Even More

No sooner had John and I moved the first furnishings into Hazel Avenue than he hits the antiques trail. He starts hauling in objects that shine like a captive sun, gleam like a horse's flank, ring with fragility, frame seductive images.

I resist momentarily. But in the face of such wonders, I throw over my buy-light upbringing and join in.

With two of us acquiring, possessions pile up in earnest: prints and paintings from the 17th to 20th centuries; oil lamps from the 1800s; Victorian crystal cabinet and mahogany dining table that seats 20; circa-1800 Chippendale mahogany sideboard; glass-fronted walnut bookcase; seven-foot-long walnut-slab desk signed "Nakashima"; Limoges table lamp that was hiding under a coat of turquoise paint; and myriad "smalls"—gilt pill box, fragments of cast-iron fencing, yellow art glass lamps reputed to be from New Jersey ... till the 10-roomer on Hazel Avenue is full and buying comes to a stop.

Till, that is, we trade Hazel Avenue in for an 18-room house on South 42nd Street. With five apartments that we run as an inn and one large apartment that we live in, the new house opens the sluice gates of acquisition for another thirty years. After all, those rooms deserve to be furnished, and furnished with character.

From the honorable State o' Maine, at the end of our September vacations, comes a load o' bounty: hand-colored photo of Mary Todd Lincoln at a piano-forte whose keys were smaller than Mrs. Lincoln's fingers; portraits of a mid-1800s landed-gentry farm couple; tin-glazed pottery from France; crystal decanters from early 1800s America; more antique lighting fixtures, some for oil, some electrified; depictions of loons both two- and three-dimensional; a fragment of silk brocade; and things I can't recall. One September our dark green Mercury "land yacht" carries back an 80-pound limestone garden urn; a spindle headboard; four grain-painted rush-seated pine chairs; a room-size oriental rug; a painted seaman's chest; and a couple of small boulders harvested from the Maine shore. The suspension system on the land yacht is not so good after that.

A beloved antiques dealer in Flourtown, a nearby suburb, and a couple of auction houses contribute to the collection: Mainline matron painted in Italian costume; 17th century Spanish floral painting in original black and gold frame; Paris china chocolate pots; pearwood music box with brass discs; trio of bronze whale-oil lamps; matched flint glass fruit compotes; large portrait attributed to Gilbert Stuart (erroneously); small portrait of a gentleman reader; diminutive drop-leaf side table; large thread-bare plum-colored oriental rug.

With pocket change from our day jobs and realized profit from the inn business bankrolling us, we've piled up a pleasing inventory of stuff—most of it eye-appealing, but without importance to a connoisseur, and a few museum-worthy pieces mixed in. Still, underneath the warp of reveling in massive possessions lies the weft of guilt for not living light, for consuming too much—the qualm that all these hard goods will catch up with me, the fantasy that I will hang from a gallows built of my possessions.

Moving Right Along

The years pass for the house on 42nd Street, and it is now as weighed down with as many possessions as non-hoarding allows. The years pass for John and me, too, and we assume the patina of our so-called golden years. Arches fall, rotator cuffs fail, cartilage shrinks, the gyroscope of balance begins to wobble, and so on. In short, the circus of decrepitude comes to town, for both of us, and thoughts turn to lightening the load.

And lightening the load turns to the primary domicile, 42nd Street, for its cruel stairs: hauling linens to the basement for laundering and to the third floor for storage; fetching a mouse trap from the basement to a shrieking Brazilian on the third floor; replacing a smoke alarm battery in the second-floor hall; chasing a squirrel out of the basement; rehanging a mirror that fell off a wall one Sunday morning; and so on, without surcease. An elevator won't work because of mid-hallway steps on the 2d and 3d floors.

The house must go, we agree. We'll replace it with a pied-a-terre in Center City. Agreed. We'll move our primary residence to the Delaware beach house. Agreed.

I sell John on my vision of a Center-City pied-a-terre that we could probably afford: bedroom and study, at least two toilets, dining space for eight, no steps. Agreed. I also propose parting with contents that we won't need or be able to house. Agreed, at least in theory.

The old possession-lite gremlin in me—certain that the material world has been too much with me and will, by and by, do me in—rises up and leads me to propose multitudes of things to divest. John, overwhelmed by the avalanche of change that is rumbling down on us, acquiesces.

Divesture ensues: an 18th century English sterling silver tea service, unused for 30 years, to a dealer in Chadds Ford; 40 boxes of historic family documents to the Hall-Walker family archive—a community history storehouse including archives of "ordinary families"—at Bowling Green State University; rare books of poetry, Mark Twain, a couple of Lynd Ward woodcut novels, and all works Philadelphian, to a Chestnut Hill dealer; hundreds of horticulture books and magazines to our gardener; 41 boxes of books to a charity thrift shop (ninety percent were John's friends for 50 years, and he is clearly in pain).

In October, the auctioneer arrives. Again, my travel-lite troll awakens and offers more than necessary: wall art we (I) have tired of; seldom-used sterling flatware, including a rare "sandwich lifter"; sterling and Sheffield silver candlesticks; a crank Victrola filled with original 78 records; a clutch of Staffordshire animal figures; John's antique lighting collection—rope lamp, betty lamps, paper-maché kerosene lamp, the Argon whale oil lamp set, and all the rest; Asian bronze figures; silver plate flatware; a large portion of Great Aunt Helen's Spode dinner service; and scores of other objects. The trove mounts on the dining room table, and John says nothing as the auctioneer takes them away.

John Puts His Foot Down

But he is bereft. He goes off and spills out his passion in a poem on a pad of yellow-ruled paper. I've seen the pad but have yet to see the poem. I haven't asked; he hasn't offered.

Maybe his anger at losing all those treasures inspired him, for he immediately demands a real-time look at some real estate.

From the firm that is selling our house comes their rental agent —a frothy and impossibly young gay man—to show us through four apartments. Each one is within budget and—eureka!—big enough to hold every possession that's been spared the ax so far.

March 1, the date for listing the 42d Street inn-domicile, arrives abruptly. We and the broker fear that our quirky piece of real estate will go unnoticed and sell for a pittance to some bottom-feeding slumlord sneering through black mustachios. But hallelujah happens, and it sells quickly and very well.

The next day we march on the building with the apartments

that impressed us most, with their light and character and size—
the Touraine—and sign up for one of their big units. The nice rental lady predicts that it may be six or eight months before an apartment comes up.

Re-Possessed

The nice rental lady is wrong, and we end up temporizing, by
house-and-cat-sitting for friends, renting a residence hotel apartment for a few months, and living at our beach home when the
summer renters aren't enjoying it.

Thirteen months later, in late September, rental lady hands us
the keys. For three days, the freight elevator brings up the stuff from
42d Street. It comes in boxes and bags, and the really big things in
their own nakedness. It is like welcoming old friends home from
a long cruise. On day three the historic gilt-brass chandelier from
42d Street, cut down a bit, is wheeled out of the elevator. From two
doors down the hall a new neighbor smiles.

By the end of the first week, almost everything is in its rightful
place: the magnificent mahogany table; the monster mohair sofas;
the 18th century Spanish still life, over the mantel and other art
where it should be; what books we still own; hundreds of pieces of
china and crystal vessels; and the rest of the cache from 42d Street.

We breathe out and know that most of our possessions are still
with us. We've lost some, held onto most. If you squint, it's as if
we've relocated 42d Street to the Touraine apartment. We almost
wallow in continuing our friendship with the old things, in reusing
them in our newest life cycle and further amortizing their cost to us
and to the planet over the course of who knows how many years to
come. Our rampant consumerism may not have been so egregious
and wasteful. I may not succumb to my possessions, after all.

A couple of weeks later, as we're rearranging Great Aunt Hel-
en's Spode china in the china cupboard for the third time, John's
face goes grey. "Where are the eared soups?" They and their service plates had long since gone to auction, and he had repressed the

fact. I dash to the computer and find an inventory of those same eared soups and under-plates at Replacements Unlimited. In fact, it is an unusually large inventory of them, all in excellent condition. There can be no doubt that twelve of those sets had been ours. I buy them back.

AWAKENINGS

27

Friendship Found, Friendship Lost

Suddenly without ballast on the ship of friends.

It was 1981. The oral surgeon had just removed two 1-inch pieces of John's lower jaw and wired his mouth shut. Above his bed was a pair of wire cutters and a sign in red Magic Marker that read "!!!Notice! If patient vomits, cut the wires!!!"

John was back home in a couple more days, and over the next ten weeks the surgeon, Otto, checked occasionally to see how the wounds were healing. By the time he took the wires out, John and Otto were friends. John invited him to our upcoming Christmas party, which at that time was bifurcated—gay edition on Friday, straight edition on Saturday. John gave Otto a choice of evening, implying that we could care less as to Otto's genderish leanings. He chose Friday and brought his partner, Jimmy.

Ten years later, Otto's relationship with Jimmy had gone south. The next, with Charles, dissolved after about 3 years. Then came several years of fruitless attempts at connecting. Eventually Mark strolled onto the scene. After a couple of dates, he and Otto became a couple.

Nor could we have wanted better for Otto. Mark was a health-care professional and an academic, and handsome, tall, and toned.

He spoke with a standard Australian accent, which sounds enough like British to cause most Americans to go moist. And he boiled over with humor and an encyclopedic store of jokes. What wasn't apparent was that he was very ill, and that wasn't revealed to us for several months.

In short order, Mark tossed another ingredient into the friendship soup: Tien Ngo. Mark lived upstairs from Fork, one of the best restaurants in town. Being too busy (too disinclined, I think) to cook, he took every meal possible at the restaurant or its take-away-food annex, and bonded with the executive chef, Tien Ngo. Mark and Otto frequently partook of the Wednesday night Chef's Tasting Menu at Fork, and one week John and I joined them: 20 foodies at a big table feasting on a fixed gourmet menu and top-shelf wines, for 40 bucks, what a deal!

Tien—tiny, wiry, of uncertain age—stepped out of the kitchen before the meal began, a short black chef's cap on his shaved pate, dressed in standard white chef's jacket and black-and-white checkered chef's pants. He greeted us in excellent English, with a light Asian accent. He comped us champagne, smiled and laughed at everything, and gushed over his friends Otto and Mark: "I love these guys."

John and I began to eat at Fork frequently on Wednesdays, usually joined by Mark and Otto at the big table. Tien would come out of the kitchen and give us some time. He would annotate the four courses for the evening and garnish them with morsels of his life. We began piecing together his story like a jigsaw puzzle—impressionistic pieces, with shifting edges, and in no particular order. Many of the pieces were funny, or had funny parts, and he delivered them like stand-up routines. A couple of the episodes were tragic. The pieces rarely fit together and there were huge gaps in the puzzle—but he was revealing an extraordinarily varied life, and voids and incongruities seemed a natural part of his story.

As we learned from him, Tien began life in a Vietnamese orphanage. He was a runt and sickly looking: not prime adoption material. In his middle teens he broke down in front of the matron of the orphanage, sobbing that he was so undesirable that he would never get adopted. The woman said something like, "Shut up! Quit your whining. I adopted you last year."

In his late teens, equipped with his pride of adoption, he left the orphanage and became a self-sufficient adult. We don't know how he made a living. Somewhere along the line he acquired a wife and children. They were killed during the Vietnamese War while he was out of the country; at whose hands they died we never learned. He nurtured the Buddhism of his upbringing to assuage his grief. Eventually, Europe became his home. He earned his PhD in French literature, published some poetry, and became a chef. After several years in Europe, mostly France, and still unsettled, he came to the States. He never mentioned a love interest after his wife.

About seven years before we met him Tien showed up at the doorsteps of Fork where owner Ellen Yin hired him as a cooks' assistant. He was competent and imaginative in all phases of the kitchen. Soon, Ellen named him executive chef, and when she published the Fork cookbook a couple of years later, virtually all the recipes were his. Tien brought his adoptive mother to Philadelphia and set her up in an apartment downtown. She and Ellen's Chinese-born mother became good friends. Tien drove them to doctors' appointments and restaurants.

Contacts escalated. Otto and Mark threw a few large dinner parties in Fork's banquet room for one celebration or another and Tien concocted the menus. One was an exuberant fruits de mer: gigantic silver epergnes of clams, oysters, crab claws, lobster halves, shrimp, and scallops. One party featured two roasted suckling pigs, to which Tien added my appetizer suggestion of Chablis sorbet and crackling skin.

Then Tien began hosting two or more of us—Otto, Mark, John, me—to dinners and lunches at Fork. I don't know if he paid for it or the restaurant did, but we went along with it happily. One feast comprised whole Dungeness crabs, halves of Maine lobster, and a hundred oysters on the half-shell. He threw a dinner to welcome John's niece to town, and another for a friend of ours from the West Coast. We were established friends of Tien, and at that point Fork was the venue of the friendship.

There was always Veuve Clicquot, the signature champagne of Otto, Mark, and Tien, and massive amounts of good red Bordeaux, which Tien drank constantly. (Tien told us his doctor limited him to two glasses of wine a day. "Mama Mia," he said. "I went out and bought a wine glass that will hold a whole bottle of wine.")

Once, when the wine was flowing, Tien threw down a startling piece of his puzzle: some years earlier (chronology uncertain) he befriended a wealthy older man, in the US, who had a physically disabled daughter. Tien became her caregiver, at least part time. Eventually, the father died and left his fortune to Tien on the condition that Tien care for the daughter. Tien did. A few years later the daughter died, and the fortune was all his. On one even more wine-saturated evening, Tien hinted that he was worth in the environs of 14 million dollars. Later, at the time the US government was pressuring Switzerland to divulge details about the holders of secret Swiss bank accounts, Tien fretted that his money was in such an account and that he could be thrown in jail. We dismissed the idea as paranoid. Tien could be a little theatrical. As usual, we didn't probe, just received the stories as delivered.

The friendship took another step up when we started meeting outside Fork. Tien treated the four of us to dinner at a Korean restaurant, where we charcoal-grilled steak and pork and beef tongue at the table. Tien brought a jeroboam of fine Bordeaux.

Another time, he hauled a cooler of oysters and striped bass and bottles of Veuve Clicquot and Bordeaux to Otto's house in Rehoboth Beach and cooked dinner for five of us. He got so drunk he curdled the hollandaise sauce and couldn't follow through with the standard chef's trick to resuscitate it.

One day he showed up at John's and my house with a fine piece of calligraphy, in Vietnamese—his own—that he had framed in clear maple. It translated as something like "The viewer is as much creator of the art as the artist."

We began including him in dinners and celebrations in our homes, including Thanksgiving. Often his restaurant schedule kept him away; but he managed to show up now and then. A friend of the first water.

Tien began talking about flying the five of us to his little village in central Vietnam in January, where he had moved as an adult and where he was preparing to become village chief when he retired.

He was probably around 60 years old. We couldn't imagine him leaving Fork, as it seemed to be 95 percent of his life. He spent 16 to 18 hours a day working there and often slept in his office. Once a year he fasted from wine for a week. The only "vacation" he mentioned was an annual trip to the Poconos. He would hire a limo to deliver him to a mountaintop, where he meditated, killed a squirrel with a slingshot and roasted it over a campfire, and slept overnight in a hammock slung between two trees. The limo driver picked him up the next morning.

The only people we knew Tien to be attached to were his mother, the four of us, Ellen and her mother, and a young couple who once worked for him at Fork and whose young daughter he godfathered. His mother had died the year before; perhaps that freed him to contemplate retiring and enjoying his wealth and returning to Vietnam and France.

"They'll have a big festival to welcome us," he told us, reveling in introducing his four American friends to his village people. "They'll slaughter a pig in front of you, and you have to watch, it's an honor. You can wear sunglasses if you want. And, Mamma Mia, make sure you don't eat anything that I don't eat first, so you don't get the Montezuma revenge." To prep us for the trip, he twice took John and me to his favorite Vietnamese restaurant, Pham, and to a Chinese restaurant with tanks of live crabs and frogs awaiting the honor of being food. He said he'd rent a Lear jet for our trip and would cover all costs. That kind of largesse, with no reciprocity on our part, embarrassed John and me; but we overcame our inclination to guilt and accepted it as recompense for our company, as he seemed to have few friends to socialize with, and as he claimed to be filthy rich. If he wanted to blow a small part of a fortune that way, who were we to deny him? We were good friends, after all.

The January of Tien's trip was several months away, but neither plans nor particulars for it were forthcoming, so John and I committed to visit friends in New Zealand in February. We were half hoping that another long flight, to Vietnam, wouldn't eventuate that year. Then Tien told us he had given Ellen notice that he was quitting after Christmas, and Vietnam suddenly got real again.

But January came and January went and Tien was still working. Ellen hadn't found a replacement, so he had stayed on. The excursion to Tien's village faded. He stopped talking about it. He still referred to retirement and said that he was going to return to Ellen all eleven years of his salary. He was very fond of her, even though they occasionally fought pitched battles over things culinary.

When Mark and Otto met, Mark, so full of life, was also full of death: fourth-stage cancer, lung and brain. He experimented with customized chemo cocktails and triangulated radiation. Tien's Buddhist friends prescribed healing rituals for his adored friend. Mark probably gained an extra four years of life, but eventually neither the physical nor the metaphysical worked. By the end of February, Mark peered through his optimism and saw that he was, as draftees say, short. He flew to Australia for a farewell tour of the familiar: family, friends, surfing sites, pubs, peninsulas, woods, deserts. Otto stayed behind to keep his surgical practice going and monitored Mark's health by phone. Toward the end of two months, Mark called from a hospital in Melbourne and asked, "How'd you like a little visit to Australia?" Tien escorted Otto to the Newark Airport, both in tears. Mark died while Otto was waiting for the flight.

Ellen took Tien's threat to retire as just another outburst of histrionics and dismissed the idea. But in March, he informed her that June was his last month, replacement or not. That got Ellen hopping, and she found a new chef, a highly credentialed one, and French, and she hired him. When Tien learned that she was going to pay the new chef more than she paid him, Tien pitched a fit. He told Ellen the restaurant would tank if she hired that man, that she should withdraw the offer, and that he, Tien, was withdrawing his resignation and returning to Fork.

As a riposte, Ellen threw a lavish retirement dinner for Tien with a hundred friends and favorite customers. We ate well, drank well, sang Hail to the Chef, and saw Tien into unemployment.

Within a couple of weeks—I assume it was for lack of something to do, as he seemed to have no life but the cooking life—he took a part-time job as sous-chef nearby. The owner wanted someone to keep an eye on the executive chef, his feckless son. There were hints of father and son connections to the mob—but so says every gossip of anyone within two blocks of South Philadelphia.

John and I and Otto continued to go to Fork, to see Ellen (who had become a friend) and to test out the new chef. Of course, we didn't see Tien there, and our out-of-Fork experiences with him began to dwindle.

Tien had earlier revealed that he had a small pension from France from years of working there, and that he would have to go to Paris soon to collect it, or lose it. One evening, he called Otto from New York to report that he had been mugged after dinner in Little Italy. He always carried a bundle of cash, for that's all he used; in this case, it was his bankroll for Paris, and the flight was the next day. Otto wired him 5,000 dollars.

The next day, at JFK Airport, Tien had an anxiety attack at the boarding gate and collapsed. He came back to Philadelphia, moved into a vacant room of a former Fork customer's condo and resumed his part-time cheffing job at the putatively mob-linked restaurant.

It was about a year after Mark died. Otto had planned a colossal 60th birthday party for himself—treating 13 of his closest friends (Tien included) to a weekend in New York, with a luxury hotel, a chef's lunch at the Gramercy Tavern, a show, and a chef-designed dinner at Per Se. Out of love for Otto and Mark, Tien offered to throw a lavish birthday dinner in Philadelphia the evening before we limoed up to the city. Tien would go to Paris when the celebratory shouting had died down.

After his New York mugging and collapse, Tien had been answering his cell phone less. By the time Otto's birthday was a week away, none of us—not even Ellen or her mother—could raise him. Tien and his pre-birthday dinner party never materialized.

The weekend in New York was sumptuous. Between measures of indulgence and hilarity the revelers awakened individually to the commanding fact that Mark wasn't among us. Otto didn't mention Mark, but behind Otto's celebratory demeanor hovered Mark's poignant silhouette. Then there was Tien. No one missed him beyond noting that he didn't show up—except his close friends, John and me and Otto. For Otto, Tien had become a metaphor for Mark, since Tien and Mark were so close. Tien's absence from the weekend amplified Mark's.

I began to view Tien as missing in action. We asked around. One of us phoned the young couple with the goddaughter, near whom Tien was planning to relocate, in Chicago. They had no idea of his whereabouts. Ellen said that when she talked to him last, Tien was getting ready for that trip to Paris. She then discovered he had borrowed money from people who worked for him at the restaurant and from the couple he was living with. He had still not repaid any of Otto's $5,000 loan

Ellen's mother took Tien's recorded message on his still-active cell phone as a sign that he would return shortly from wherever he had gone. But the rest of us advanced to the worry state: did the mob of his new restaurant do him in? Was he mugged for his ever-present bankroll and his diminutive body shoved down a sewer? Did he escape to Paris to pick up his pension and perhaps mega-bucks from his Swiss account?

Then we began reviewing the jigsaw puzzle of his life, gnawing over which pieces were true—even the piece that was his name. We looked at ourselves open-mouthed as we realized how many gaps remained in the puzzle of Tien and at how we never tried to fill them in; how greedily we had accepted Tien's genuineness; how passive we were in corroborating his stories through their mere acceptance by others, like Ellen and Mark.

How flimsy were the stories from which we befriended him. One or two verifiable features, like the realness of Ellen's mother or the fact that Ellen met Tien's mother, were authentication enough for the other features of his history. We realized that we were as much part of the illusion of Tien as Tien himself— "The viewer is as much creator of the work of art as the artist"—and this realization only made us feel worse. In the backwash of that lost friendship bobbed the sunk cost of emotional investment.

Tien's calligraphy is sitting in the basement now, facing the furnace room wall. I'm waiting for it to glow red when Tien is ready to return.

28

Death by Art

Burly glass artist, cousin James, comes calling.

James studied glass for 12 years in Prague, where he fabricated it into windows and sculptures. On his way back to his home in New Zealand, he's decided to stop in on his American relatives across the States. John, a first cousin, one of four first cousins in the Walker-Hall family is number one on his list, east-to-west. I am meeting him for the first time.

Into our muted-sage-and-gilt Victorian vestibule he bursts, gigantic purple duffle and all. He booms, "Well, here we are, mates," and crushes us in rib-bruising man-hugs and thumps our backs. It's a theatrical entrance, the kind instantly distrusted by people at the introvert end of the Myers-Briggs scale. Which includes me. And my kin; I can't think of a single bona fide extrovert in the family. Our voices were rarely raised in anger or in zeal. Well, zeal, but only modestly raised.

I always try to lay on an impressive dinner for guests, and John ordinarily does a real dessert, which we deny ourselves when alone. This evening I put myself out more than usual for my new-found relative; but I had long since quit maintaining a menu diary, and I can't remember what it was.

James starts the dinner with a monologue, all the while smiling and eating, on his Prague years as a visiting glass artist. Then he shifts into overdrive and launches into the conversational landscape of Europolitics; American politics; contemporary culture; the Czech language; how to pretend to be Czech so the landlady won't evict the woman he was subletting from; his home in New Zealand; and topics beyond. Voluble is a synonym for James B. Walker. Garrulous is another. Even though in full logorrheic mode, he seems to be trying to open discussion or debate, and even asks about our lives and professions. But he doesn't leave enough space for response. I wonder if he talks in his sleep.

He has a slightly stilted way of speaking—not bloviating or bombastic, but almost overly clear and penetrating, and cheer-leaderish, like a good fifth-grade soccer coach. With an infusion of Aussie-Kiwi-isms like "mate" and "bloke" delivered in his mild southern Chattanooga accent, the style comes across as histrionic, rehearsed. To his credit, he interrupts himself several times to laud the food and wine.

The wine glasses are filled and refilled, and his engagement ramps up. Questions addressed to us shrink to zero and discourses became louder and less interruptible. By dessert time, my brain is barricading itself against the torrent of words and his extraordinary zest. I block out the palaver and dream of clearing away the dishes and bedtime. Thank god, he's only staying one night.

On that first visit James detected—no real trick to it, but it did show that he could attend to things beyond the boundaries of himself—that his "dear cuz" and I were a couple—which we had not shared with our families at that point. As James wended his way across the country, visiting this and that relative, he lost no opportunity to spread the news of our oneness, like an "outing" Johnny Appleseed—not from viciousness, I'm sure, but from his inability to keep anything to himself. Thus, Jameses' brother Jock knew, the other cousin, Vaughn, knew, John's brother and sister-in-law and nephews and niece knew, and the matriarch of the family,

Aunt Jane, knew. It turns out that everyone—since Uncle Jack, Aunt Jane's husband, a known homophobe, was deceased—was OK with the revelation.

We weren't sure which way James' sexual compass pointed; he made no mention of alliance or dalliance with either gender.

The next encounter with James was vicarious. On a visit to James' brother, Jock, in Portola Valley, California, we made the acquaintance of James' profession: stained glass. Jock hauled out a couple of books in which several of James' windows had been published. The actual installations were big things, created for major architectural statements in churches, university halls, and public buildings. There was a black-and-white photo of James in profile, capped with a Scottish beret of sorts, draped with a carefully arranged muffler-scarf, thrusting his well bearded chin upward, for burly drama, to one of his major installations. A few of the creations in the book he had reproduced in miniature, and they were hanging in Jock's large picture windows.

The designs were chiefly broken lines, acute angles, sequences of bars, and jagged ribbons, sometimes laid out in geometric progression, pacing from side to side and top to bottom, like a page from an alien manuscript, and sometimes exploding into a solid color field caught in lazy, curvy lines. The colors were bold, favoring red, black, white, and clear. They were totally to my taste. James' art mirrored his enthusiasm, the rhythm of his prolixity, the masculinity of his unquenchable energy. It began to de-ice my distrust and disaffection.

A couple of years later, we encountered James again in Portola Valley, again at Jock's home, but this time in the flesh. John had convinced me that we were spending an inordinate amount of time with my family and ignoring his; so we were visiting again, deliberately close to the last visit. James happened to pop in from New Zealand to promote his current glass art, the outcome of his years in Prague: glass sculpture. He set a few objects in front of us: a piece of nearly two-dimensional glass spires that looked like the ups and downs of the Dow-Jones average and ranged from red-orange through sunny yellow; and several sculptures, some purple, some green, of solid glass cylinders intersecting with other solid-geometric forms. Over dinner, he glossed the objects in a steady stream of verbiage, like an over-excited puppy. As dinner came to an end, the art well ran dry. But James did not. As Jock, John, Yuriko (Jock's wife) and I drew in breath in anticipation of saying something, James' well of other topics overflowed, and each sip of after-dinner drink raised his word-flow and volume to the point where we all retired to bed out of self-defense.

James' adoptive New Zealand is utopia to many people. It has some of the youngest geography on the globe—unsettled, like shifting land, erupting volcanoes, and dramatic water features and craggily wondrous mountainscapes. Its civil rights are highly evolved—the first nation to give women the vote, for example, and an enviable record of including multiple races and gays (with historic lapses with the Maori and the Chinese). The people are close to the earth: no one seems to be more than one degree of separation from farm life—yet civilization is high enough to turn out very good chocolate croissants, world-class sauvignon blancs, creative "new" cuisine, and good classical music.

New Zealand politics are utopian enough that, in the midst of the George W. Bush regime, John and I thought of joining the imagined and largely unpopulated diaspora. When our assessment of America's political futures was at its nadir—little did we imagine that worse was yet to come—expatriating to NZ was a frequent topic of dinner conversations between us.

But we got a grip on reality and, in 2008, as Hillary and Barack were mudwrestling through the primaries on the way to replacing Bush, we decided to visit friends in Auckland and cousin James in Waiora. On hearing our plans, James phoned John. "Cuz, yer too old for that flight," he said. (He was only six and eight years younger than we.) But we went anyhow, and in the middle of our stay with the Auckland friends, flew to the east coast for a few days with James.

He met us at the Napier airport with his big grin and "Howdy, mates." A few miles out of the airport, he stopped to uncork a choice regional Sauvignon Blanc, our welcome to his portion of our visit. An hour and a half later, John and I had finished the wine—James abstained—and we were parked at his one-story five-room white bungalow in Waiora, on the northern coast of Hawkes Bay.

In the course of our three days, James showed off the town's newly renovated 1930s movie palace; introduced us like trophies to local friends—a Maori antique dealer and the movie projectionist, and a few others; transported us up a mountainous state park to what was thought to be the nation's oldest rata tree (800-1000 years); led us along a wild beach to collect pumice and shells; drove us south, to Cape Kidnapper, to spend a night at his friend Suzy's home that sat flat on the sandy shore of the Pacific.

All with his usual passion. He lived a life of exclamation points.

Also regarding passion: we guessed that Suzy was or had been somewhat more than a friend; it was easy to see the allure of a blond model, even through a bit of middle-aged avoir du pois.

Most important in the whole visit, James unveiled his recent art. Some was standing around or hanging around his house; some had to be pulled out of cushioned packing crates: modern, weighty glass sculptures that we had sampled in the states, and his recent Chevron series—painted, pounded panels of fire-safety glass.

As he rattled on about the pieces, we heard more of his story. James came to art late. He got a Bachelor of Science degree in marketing in the States. After he fell in love with and immigrated to New Zealand, he took a Master's in fine arts. Moving through a series of apprenticeships and master classes he ended up a noted fabricator of stained-glass windows. (Our Auckland friends, academics at the University, worked alongside a couple of his major windows in their office buildings; and we saw another at a local Christian Science Church.)

James's art came in a rugged frame, that of a large and fairly bulky man, a man of simple movement and the rarest moment of pretention. A fully-testosteroned fellow, it seemed. His art was, too. In showing his work, his words were of the "this was fun," "...great color," "I really like dealing with big chunks of glass" sort; not the "inner light of a sphere of glass is..." or "the crags on this radiate to the celestial, like the spires of a church..." (though they did).

He made art through increments and happy accidents—not unlike many other artists, but very James in the simplicity of his approach. He addressed the material, much of it found stuff, like safety glass and tractor tires, as challenges, a joyous, noisy confrontation between it and him that he could win by wresting from it a piece of art—like the Chevron series, for which he painted yellow and black chevrons on strips of fire-safety glass, then hammered it selectively till here only wires showed, there shards of glass hanging by the wires, and yet there stretches of untouched glass.

That was James. Exuberant in all things—in his art, in his loves, in a glass of wine, several glasses of wine, in connecting with relatives and even a relative by "marriage" (me); exuberant in climbing a mountain; exuberant in showcasing his adoptive New Zealand.

And there was me, of calm demeanor, light on expressed emotion. So practiced in passive restraint that I could have been a Volvo air bag. Phlegmatic. James was almost always in the company of others when I was around. We had very few opportunities to delve into each other as he was leaping from topic to topic and I was—perhaps—finding the company of others a way to avoid serious engagement. But there I was, nonetheless, face to face with James the Exuberant—my pale-passioned yin contemplating his outrageous yang, and absorbing it. Not to the point of recasting me in his mold, but of complementing my calm and pensive take on life with a resonance toward an emotionally other, temperamentally other soul.

✳ ✳ ✳

At the time, John and I didn't realize that James the artistic was waxing—that his work, old and new—the modernist stained-glass windows, the pure and simple glass sculptures—was gaining traction in the art glass community—beginning to break into the sanctity of museum preserves. Nor did we, or he, realize that James the corporeal was waning rapidly, from mesothelioma contracted years ago, probably while cutting asbestos for his art before one could know better. His presenting illness was relatively short. He shouldered through it with his usual bravado and exuberance, strong enough to exalt in bestowing his significant instance of art on humankind; and strong enough to have Suzy's daughter DNA-tested and shout out that he had given the world a daughter.

Three years after our visit, generous, untamable, gifted, and deeply loved James B. Walker died, at age 63.

29

Shaking Faith

How to stop worrying and love the Big Bang.

We come into the world godless. On top of that, we know it. When we pop out of that dark, warm, wet primal nest into the glaring reality of the birthing room, our budding brains must know that no thing of goodness had a hand in such an act. A properly beneficent deity would have devised a less cruel way of being born, maybe even a fun way, like conception.

Regardless, we are born and we are immediately of the world, as religion of one stripe or another rushes in to stake its claim. Before our tiny beings have a chance to consider the alternatives, faith-crazed adults put us in a belief-system hammerlock with a creation myth, a text of murky lessons and rules that are inviolable and, often, a story line of a superhero of unnatural birth who becomes or subs for a deity.

The grownups wage their belief system with an intensity that can range from sadistic to suffocating to gentle. My grandparents on both sides and my parents were anything but zealots, and it followed that my parents laid religion on me gently.

Gently, but without choice or debate on my part.

My mother was raised Christian Scientist; my father, northern

Baptist, not as rabid as the southern variety. I was baptized in the first few months of life; but I don't remember the denomination of the church, and I can't find a record of it—but it wasn't a Christian Science event, because they have no such rite.

After our family left West Virginia for Ohio—I was six—Dad converted to Methodism because the Methodist church choir was the best in town, and he enjoyed singing with them. I attended Methodist Sunday school when we first moved to town. I remember that the building looked and felt warm and churchy—gabled and steepled red brick pierced by pointed stained-glass windows depicting stories from the Bible—and that groups of women organized pot luck dinners in the basement. I vaguely recall gathering with an adult on Sunday morning amongst pastel-colored posters of Biblical stories and talking about things related to the Bible.

Within a year, my mother reversed my religious fortune and hauled me off to the First Church of Christ, Scientist. It didn't look churchy. It looked like someone's town house, which is what it had been. On Sunday morning, opening services were held in a large off-white room upstairs—probably a master bedroom suite. Everyone, adults and children, gathered to recite The Lord's Prayer and The Scientific Statement of Being ("There is no life, truth, intelligence, nor substance in matter. All is infinite Mind and its infinite manifestation, for God is All-in-all. Spirit is immortal Truth; matter is mortal error. Spirit is the real and eternal; matter is the unreal and temporal. Spirit is God, and man is His image and likeness. Therefore man is not material; he is spiritual.") and sing hymns.

Then the adults went down to what had been the living and dining rooms, also off-white, to hear readings from the Old and New Testaments and from *Science and Health, with a Key to the Scriptures* by Mrs. Eddy. The children stayed on the second floor and adjourned in age-clustered groups to small off-white rooms for Sunday school.

I don't remember any Sunday school teacher before I was 12 or so. At that point Mrs. Nan Savage materialized. The Sunday lessons consisted of discussing some of the readings that the adults were hearing downstairs. Given the intellectual and Zen-like nature of Christian Science, it was natural for the discussions to turn to broad issues of life, belief, and philosophy as we children struggled to reconcile the unreal material universe with the real spiritual one as we sought to Believe.

Most religions navigate the countervailing forces of good and evil. For Christian Scientists this boils down to fending off the magnetic pull of the material away from the spiritual. In the public mind, this takes its most palpable form as denying themselves medical care. But even to the vast majority of the CS faithful, certain material matters don't respond well to the power of Mind. Dentistry and optometry probably account for the most common CS acknowledgements of the sway of the material world.

Mrs. Nan Savage had long since come to grips with the conundrum of the faith and professed infinite Mind to be all. But she, like other faithful, seemed unable to escape entirely the grip of the physical. She may or may not have succumbed to dentists, and she didn't wear glasses. But it was clear to me from the beginning that she was accepting enough of the material universe to make an elegant appearance—tailored outfits that set off her small, trim figure and coifed black hair, and always gloves—of which she never removed the right one. She enjoyed other benefits of the physical, like being well-heeled. (Not uncommon among CS congregants, generally. Our family was probably in the lowest economic percentile.) These characteristics did not smack of Spirit to me and seemed inconsistent with what the religion was all about.

Mrs. Nan Savage once treated the Sunday school class to lunch at her big white house. The maid answered the door and let us into a huge marble foyer. Mrs. Nan Savage swept in from another room—gloveless—and rushed to a little box on a side table where she picked up something and worked it onto her right hand. It was a digit-and-a-half's worth of artificial finger. More of that pesky materiality.

Hostess-teacher and children finished our grown-up lunch of something or other good (today it might have been chicken salad with pineapple chunks and almonds, alongside asparagus spears). Hostess-teacher rang a crystal bell, and a wide female servant in a bright white apron, probably the cook, served us scoops of vanilla iced cream from a cut crystal bowl, as we sat with our hands in our laps. It was my earliest brush with the high side of Matter, and I was impressed. Surely, at some future date I would find a way to piece it together with Mind and Spirit.

When I finished high school, my family moved to a suburb of Washington, DC. There, out of passivity and habit, I continued with CS Sunday school. For a short while, the leader was a Mrs. Henson; then, for a slightly longer while, her son Jim (yes, the same creator of the Muppets playing a different role with me); then the admirable Mrs. Emerson, who dressed modestly and taught speech and elocution at the local 4-H Club and seemed altogether down to earth. As a side benefit, she tutored us in how to read out loud— which I drew on later in lecturing and public presentations. On the point of the faith, she welcomed tough questions about the religion. Many were challenges from me: Is any knuckling under to the material—say, taking an aspirin—a sin? If there's no reality in the physical, why has no one in the history of the religion demonstrated conquering certain physical failings (vision, teeth, lost limbs) through Mind? Isn't the death of our physical body an admission of its reality? And so on.)

At age 20, a CSer graduates from Sunday School to adult church services. After my 20th birthday, I attended a handful of these, which amounted to hymns and selected reading from the Bible and the *Science and Health*, and testimony of prayerful "healings" that any congregant volunteered. No discussion, no debate.

And "no more," I announced to Mom. Thus ended my religious practice. Mom saw it coming and didn't react, and Dad took no notice. I think he understood.

But the thought of a religious affiliation lingered on, because it was such a big deal to everyone outside myself—the warp, if not also the weft, of the social fabric. I pondered one religion after another, from Buddhism to Judaism and back again. I struggled with each of them, not in deep, sweating wrestling bouts, but in light sparring: tap, pat, tap, pat, I poke you, you poke me. I was looking for substantiation. Show me. Prove it. Make me say, "Oh yeah, that's it. That's why the claims are true. That's why I know these things to be the case, why I can say out loud that the deity *is* and that claims to the contrary are false."

I became a religious outlier. Everyone I knew had a religious label; I had none. As time went by, I tagged myself Agnostic. When asked what my faith was—which people did and still do with the assumption that you must have one—I usually responded that I had none. In the army, when the top sergeant had each of us shout out our religions, I shouted out Methodist. Boot camp didn't seem the place to challenge society's insistence on theism, and certainly no place to bring up an inexplicable cult like Christian Science. Besides, I had given that up.

Life continued, as it does, one damn thing after another. Now and then a gift out of nowhere or a coincidence came along that was too preposterous or too precious or too eery: I received a generous federal fellowship for my doctoral studies without applying for it; my first glacier, in Alaska, revealed dazzling blue and green jewels locked inside; I dreamed of a high school friend at the same time my mother, on the other side of the country, was writing to tell me he had been killed in Vietnam. At such moments, I, a fatalist, a liver of life in the passive lane, a mote tossed about in the tornadoes of probability, looked for explanation. Wasn't there something akin to preordination, or semi-intelligent design, a Big Jokester in the Sky, even, or some omnipotent force given to a taste for beauty, ugliness, and gross sarcasm?

A couple of decades slipped by. When I was 43, my mother died in St. Petersburg, Florida. We held a Christian Science memorial service in the funeral home. Later, that day or the next, my father and my cousin Carol and I were in Dad's living room, having a drink. Our conversation turned to Mom and the service and death and, finally, faith. I averred that I was a non-believer. My cousin and my father—my Baptist-raised, hymn-loving father—confessed to agnosticism. I was ready to agree, when it occurred to me that I no longer was in doubt about the existence of a deity. I had but one question, and I had its answer: "Is there any irrefutable evidence in support of a deity?" "No."

Over the next 30 years my brand of atheism evolved from not believing in one or another deity to certainty that there is no deity to believe in. My personal Scientific Statement of Being ran: "All is Universe and its infinite Probabilities."

By and large, my atheism has posed only miniscule problems—I am perennially angry at the bald-faced presence of religion in American public life; I squirm in the company of faith-based zealots; I feel sad when people whose intellects I respect avow a faith; I wince at my own hypocrisy when I haul out the Christmas tree decorations every year, and can't wait till I can stop, without fear that my other half, a devotee of Christmas decoration, would kick me out of the house.

The Big Atheist Problem for me is, or will be, death. In order to deny the undeniable—death—our species has developed myriad scenarios of after-life existence, where we, or certain anointed, anyhow, continue to exist; and where—whether riding white ponies up to a celestial harem of virgins or floating in the ether as disembodied Mind—there is a distinct improvement over our time on earth.

Absent an after-life destination, what's to comfort one in those snoozy, anxiety-ridden early morning hours when thoughts naturally turn to death? In light dreams I see me as a lonesome juggernaut—a juggernaut of my own being. On aging limbs I inch toward the void, crushing everything in my path—big-deal things, like time and space, and eventually the small-deal thing, my own self. I have no belief system that I can draw on with a straight face to ameliorate the trip to the edge. And, when it comes time to exit, there is no force to deliver me to an ethereal landscape or to harbor my disembodied spirit. My mind processes down that storied black tunnel to a beneficent-seeming light at the end—or is it a door, off white, with raised panels? I move through the utopic and the hellish—bucolic meadows, Bruegelish purgatories, French tulips, Mrs. Nan Savage's artificial finger, ogres, Muppets, my mother's face in green, my father's violin in purple, a protestant hymn in crimson, a croissant inset with diamonds—all from my own misfiring nervous system—and understand that when the snap lock on the door of death clicks behind me, there will be nothing, not even me, on the other side.

30

Not My Own High School Reunion

In the flatlands of Northwest Ohio John bravely debuts his significant other (me) to his classmates of 1960.

A hundred and fifty years ago, Bowling Green was part of the Great Black Swamp, before human beings happened and drained the swamp and uncovered in the northwestern corner of Ohio about 1,500 square miles of dark, rich farmland.

Swamp or farmland, it was and is unapologetically flat, stretching off into infinity like a Dalí landscape. To a hill-hugging boy from southern Ohio, infinity is a forlorn and scary vista, made scarier by country roads no wider than double golf carts, berm-free, hemmed in by grassy drainage trenches that could swallow a minivan, and lacking even the illusion of safety that a guard rail could convey. Along these roads we hurtle, toward the 40th anniversary celebration of the Bowling Green High School Class of 1960, John's 40th high school reunion.

I'm sure that John's classmates would have adored him in high school, and would still today. I've witnessed near-total strangers call him "Huggy Bear" and the like and, at the Y, one woman holler his name across the aerobics room just to see him smile. It's this adored, smiley, Huggy-Bear man that I'm with. So where does my case of nerves come from? For one, I've never met his classmates and, for a fundamentally introverted person heading into a weekend-long party with strangers, that itself carries a weighty payload of tension. And what if introducing his significant other—a man—me—turns out to be such a miscalculation that we reap social opprobrium or a bloody nose or death in one of those bottomless drainage ditches? I don't really believe the death option. But after all, we're in the heartland, and in 2000 AD public opinion about gay people is pretty evenly divided. On top of that, the social failing of my own high school experience was, on its own, enough to raise high (-school) anxiety.

The day before, we drive in from Philadelphia a day early, check into our motel, and head to dinner with Doris and Patricia, friends of John's parents. Maggie's "family restaurant," one of their favorites, is a large dark cave with faux walnut walls and tables accented by plastic philodendrons. Tonight it's pretty empty—none of the screaming babies that "family" implies, just a few sullen teenagers and their double-wide parents. The food is ironic, unfortunately a common American idiom: in the midst of rich farm country, at the end of July, a salad of old lettuce and pale plastic tomatoes and a side of green beans from a can, boiled to a grey mush. The strip steak is OK. Doris says "These beans are good." Patricia agrees. We are in the land of bad food.

The next night the reunion begins. John and I drive to the small antique-car museum on the edge of town. John precedes me and opens the door to a tableau—a freeze-frame of 58-year-old faces fixed on us. Action resumes quickly, and 20 or so late-middle-agers fall all over themselves rushing to hug John (the men do manly back-pats) and Jan and Kathy and Bill and Chris the woman and Chris the man and Reenie and so on introduce themselves to me. John knows them all, of course, and I know none, of course, and their names evaporate before they reach my ears. Someone gives me a name tag and a photo to pin on my coat. The name tag says "I'm with ..." ; an arrow points to a year-book photo of John. All the spouses have similar IDs.

His classmates all seem eager to meet the mysterious, significantly other me—the partner of perennially partnerless John. Actually, I'm not that mysterious, for John has set them up with my background and has probably been preparing them for this encounter for some years. And it shows: everyone, man and woman, is aggressively friendly and welcoming. As a mind can do when over-excited, mine spasms to several realizations all at once: that John's the only known gay person in his class, that these classmates are all remarkably close to each other, and that every female in his class had a crush on John Hall back in the day.

Forty-two years before, in a small town at the other end of Ohio, my tenure in Chillicothe High School, with the Class of 1958, was about to end. My experience there had been about 180 degrees from John's. For four years I was a focused student, almost nerd-like, too recessive a personality, perhaps seen as queer or potentially so. I was window glass to virtually all other classmates, not even worth the attention and effort required for bullying. The few friends I had were fringe-ers, too, outside the social mainstream and not even good stock on which to practice the art of being a friend. I think none of us knew what friending was all about. Late in my senior year I established light, hobbled relationships with a few who were interesting and also college bound, but there wasn't time enough to create real bonds. Or maybe I didn't have the will to bond, suffering, as I view it, from a genetic complaint handed down by my father. In a taxonomy of personality disorders it might be known as Fear of Acceptance, manifested in the conviction that friendship could lead to entanglements that would, upon a kindness being extended to one, obligate one to reciprocities that would likely be distasteful or discommodating; a conviction that friendship will coerce one into doing things one would rather not do, like house their dog for a month or sharpen the blades of their lawn mower.

The day after I graduated, my family moved from unprepossessing Chillicothe to culturally, gastronomically, and socially wondrous Washington, DC. A year after the move, in the seductive light of college and the big city, my last thin friendships of high school had evanesced.

Probably 50 years later, I found myself on an email list of CHS alums. A classmate whom I couldn't remember mistook me for another Thomas Childers whose writings she admired and wrote to share some highlights of her life since commencement. I shared back, including my same-sex commitment. Within days some power broker of the CHS Class of '58 had expunged me from the list of alums—for that disclosure, I am sure—tossed me into the CHS memory hole.

On the second day of John's reunion, midafternoon, we convene in a downtown theater, where the class airs a short film about the class of 1960—a collage of still photos with captions. There are glimpses of John in this or that photo, and I get to know his classmates a little, in their classmate personae. Charlie, one of the organizers, announces that 80 astounding percent of the living graduates of the Class of 1960 have signed up for this reunion.

The centerpiece of the weekend is the big dinner that evening. We gather near the main town park, in an Independent Order of Odd Fellows hall. A few decorations make it festive, and the mood is vibrant. The food, as I could now predict, is bad. I sit next to Sidney, an alumna who had just flown in from Dallas—a glamorous, witty, sophisticated woman devoid of small-town or bumpkin persona. We exchange our Texas and east-coast bios and bond over the desiccated chicken.

The morning of the next and final day, we all troop into the banquet lodge in the city park. Several of the men—yesteryear's BMOCs, even the football star—cook a farewell breakfast. The food isn't gourmet, but at last, in this land of bad food, it's good. And in the realm of matters that matter, there is unescapable evidence of group love among the Class of 1960—strong positive regard for each other, from the class stars to the class ordinaries, even to those with terminally quirky traits and blatant peccadilloes, and especially to those who have suffered in any way since graduation.

To one with a dysfunctional high school past and an outcast present, the group glows with all those fine positive feelings. Breakfast for me consists of eggs and bacon and awe and envy. I wonder where my high school culture went and why I wasn't there with it. The light goes on midway through a bite of toast, and it dawns on me that the BGHS Class of 1960 has adopted me and has broken the curse, overridden the denial of my own high school birthright. I am—goddamn!—a member of a high school class.

31

Dialogues with My Humanist Self

Mixing religious oil and secular water.

The first time I experienced a live production of Poulenc's *Dialogues des Carmelites*, at the Met, I was stunned. When the lights came up, I gathered up my senses and staggered out into the night. I'd been prepared for a snarl of feelings. Listening to the LP several times, the opera—a tale retold through the aeons, of the ultimate sacrifice for a higher cause—never failed to overwhelm me.

But from the live stage, the famous final scene—14 nuns filing toward the guillotine, their celestial hymn of martyrdom punctuated by random-seeming THWACKs and diminishing voice by voice, till silence swallows the final note—scrambled my emotions. My face had to have been a mask of woe, for others' were, too. The upwelling in my eyes showed in theirs, and lumps like the one in my throat must have been in theirs.

John and I met our two Philadelphia friends on the plaza out front. As we composed our feelings, we were also trying to figure out how to get back to Philadelphia. The trains were no longer running because, minutes before the performance was to start, a tear-gas canister had been set off in a backstage elevator in protest for or against (I forget which) Puerto Rican statehood. This led to evacuating the audience, which led to an hour's delay in the opera's finish. It also probably heightened everyone's sensibilities. It was 1977.

In the spring of 2019—again at the Met, probably the fifth time I had seen it live—I found the production to be just about as stunning as the first. But this time, out of my emotional miasma, like a message welling up in a Magic Eight-Ball, bobbed a paradox: how can a quintessentially religious opera continually evoke such strong emotions in me? And how can it be one of my favorite musical works? After all, I have eschewed, even scorned, the mythologies of religion for decades.

* * *

Living as a humanist or atheist in a society that is more religious than not can lead to complications of the soul.

As a newly admitted agnostic in my late teens I would toady to religious bullies (that is, just about anyone who said a positive word about religion) to avoid conflict or opprobrium or just plain attention. I remember as a teenage dinner guest being asked to say grace and politely demurring but, when the host finished his prayer, obediently mumbling Amen. And in Army boot camp, when the first sergeant was asking everyone to shout out their religion, I found it convenient and non-confrontational and, afterwards, craven to shout out Methodist.

By middle age, I was an avowed humanist-atheist and comfortable in that. Of course, social forces continued to tout religion, as when Congress tacked "under god" onto the Pledge of Allegiance and all levels of government and civic institutions generally ignored the correct-minded sector of the citizenry (being me and my like, of course). Now and then, some humanist-atheist victories squeaked through, like allowing children to refrain from prayer in public school and removing a monument to the Ten Commandments from a federal courthouse.

Over time, reflecting on the victories of the activist-atheists who brought them about, I realized that the least I could do would be to count myself with them, out loud—to announce my position. The world at large flaunts faith as if belief in some sort of creation legend were universal. I wanted to liberate them from that assumption, not in hope of converting others, but in some tiny way to balance the public ledger of religiousness. So, far short of marching on the tents of quaking, born-again Christians to shout down their folly, I began to pipe up now and then, in small social circles.

Nevertheless, comfortable as I am with my position and my certainty of it, and even with my piddling activism in the name of that position, I have to admit that I am stained by religious residue. The taint results largely from an upbringing and a social context that I can't or choose not to shake off completely.

I was brought up with Christmas. The warmth and fun and beauty of that holiday was an epoxy that helped weld my family foursome—Mom, Dad, my brother, and me—together. And to this day, hypocrisy aforethought, I honor Christmas by decorating to it—12-foot tree and the eight hours trimming it, green garlands, glistening ornaments, ribbon everywhere, and gigantic red and cream poinsettias. Even Christmas pudding and now and then a Christmas goose—served on the Christmas-Tree pattern of Spode china. I've taken to calling our large annual open house a Winter Party; but that's delusional. It's a Christmas party. We sometimes even have a strolling flutist playing Christmas Carols.

I try to blame my duplicity on the highly Victorian house we live in, which demands a Christmas fix once a year, and on John, who can't imagine December 25th without a serious salute to the holiday. But in reality, I persist in the lie because I enjoy the season's trappings, and the sludge of hypocrisy hasn't reached my chin, isn't yet high enough to make me stop. So I keep invoking the holiday, in body if not in spirit, waiting for the day when we leave the Christmas insistence of this house and can slough off Christmas itself, like any self-respecting atheist. Should John permit me. Or should I.

Not so two-faced is my entanglement with religious music. I

had no choice as a child but to sing along with the hymns in Sunday school or church, or even in some public meetings (scouts, commencements, and other venues). They laved something in my soul. I came to love many of them, not for their familiarity and certainly not for their words, but for their harmonic beauty and its power to lift one up. Even in my mid-twenties, when I first heard Amazing Grace, it immediately brought that familiar shudder of elevation, the kind I get when I crowd-sing the Star Spangled Banner. In my 40s, when visiting Mom and Dad, we would often sing a few hymns after dinner, exercising Dad's beautiful baritone and confident organ playing, Mom's light soprano, and my limited-scale tenor-baritone mix. The sweetness of the tunes lifted my parents, I assumed, and me, without doubt. Then Mom died, and the singing stopped, for two voices didn't seem quite enough. But more than fifteen years later, at Dad's memorial service, as the tiny and not-so-well-tuned choir launched into Rock of Ages, I collapsed in tears. Involuntary, Christian-made tears. My brother, who shares my a-religiosity, sobbed, too. Part association, part sheer beauty.

Falling somewhere between egregious contradictory behavior (my overt and deliberate Christmas infidelities) and involuntary actions (welling of emotions triggered by hymns fed to me as a child), is duplicitous preference. And I have plenty of that, in the form of classical religious music—100-percent godly, but so exquisite that I cannot deny it. So I blind myself to the text of the music—easy to do with Bach and Haydn, whose German I don't understand, and ultra-easy with some of Hovhaness's works, which are wordless. Unfortunately, the English in Handel's *Messiah* is so understandable—and totally Biblical—that I rarely listen to it. Even many years ago, when I bought a German-language CD version, thinking it would help me ignore the text, it was too late; I knew the meaning of the verses. Gradually, I left *Messiah* behind.

But *Dialogues des Carmelites*—equally religious, and abundantly clear to me in its text and story line, even though it's in French—cannot be ignored. The music alone would please me, but the sublime and tragic-heroic combo of score and book raise pleasure to adoration. In my mind's workshop I could recast the opera's tale in a secular mode—one moral cause or another that leads to martyrdom—like sacrificing oneself for others' freedom, as in Tiananmen Square, or for socio-political glory, like Nathan Hale, or, on the heels of the movie *Selma*, a reimagined *Dialogues de Birmingham 1963*, in whose final scene 14 African American teenagers file in protest into a barrage of white riot-police gunfire.

But mental gamesmanship is bootless. It doesn't lessen my heresy. So I end up arguing myself into accepting *Dialogues* existentially, receiving it as an allegory that can carry an atheist on wings of immaculate music and bitter-joyous story line out of the pit of human cruelty to the pinnacle of human glory.

That's as godless as I can make it, the best I can do.

32

On the Other Side of a Marriage Long in Coming

*After shacking up for 40 years,
does actual marriage make a difference?*

Friends, straight and gay, who had been living together for a long time before they wed, said it would be different after we got married. They were at a loss to specify what "it" was (the relationship? their psyches? life in general? who takes out the garbage?) or how the "it" differed; but they implied that the difference would be positive.

As of the previous spring, John and I had been together and committed for 39 and a half years. For most of that time, our fellow Americans had declared through assorted statutes and constitutions that people of the same gender should not have sex with each other, should not love each other, and should most certainly not enter into any formal bond, like marriage.

Many years ago, long before I had a gay pulse—or at least recognized it—I had already shrugged off the social mandate of marriage, deciding that I need not play Ken to some girl's Barbie and that if I were ever to take my place beside a curvy figure in a rose-covered suburban cottage, it would be when I was good and ready.

I finally came out some years later. My earlier brave dismissal of marriage became irrelevant, for bona fide marriage wasn't an option in the gay community. When John and I got together, we declared our commitments, in private, to each other.

That, and a jointly held mortgage or two, seemed to suffice. Year piled on year, and we stayed together, bound by interests (classical music, fine art, food), orientation to living (making a nest), choice of fun (entertaining, multitudes of friends, antiquing, European travel, music), profession (university profs), backgrounds (Ohio up-bringing close to farm roots) and, probably most important, tem-perament (conflict avoidance, civil interchange, and rapid forgiving of error, insult, and disagreement). Marriage seemed unnecessary.

As our relationship was blooming in the early 70s, the force for same-sex marriage in this country was taking baby steps. Iso-lated couples and gay rights advocates sued various states for the right to marry, and lost.[1] These forays barely registered with me; they seemed too science-fictional, too improbable in my lifetime. Even the less radical idea of mainstreaming gays into the dominant society seemed remote and even—given that many gay folk found magic in the games of dissimulation, subterfuge, and a speak-easy kind of existence—not universally desirable even among gays.

Relatively piddling levels of pressure for marriage equality con-tinued—not big and not frequent, but with enough political con-sequence that eventually the US Congress got so worried that it defined marriage as a one-woman, one-man institution in the 1996 Defense of Marriage Act (DOMA).[2] This was followed by a stream of anxious state legislatures banning same-sex unions or marriage, through statute or constitutional amendment.

Contrariwise, as the 21st century dawned, American public opinion on gays was beginning to change. The movers and shakers of gay advocacy jumped on that crescendo and turned it into a vig-orous assault on the two ultimate social peaks for gays: open service in the military and marriage.

The movement toward acceptance gained strength, and we felt steadily more enfranchised. By 2012 it became impossible for John and me to ignore the growing number of states signing on to same-sex marriage and the growing number of our gay friends who were exchanging vows legally. We began remarking on the newspaper accounts of the subject—in the abstract, bemusedly, but never as it might apply to us.

By early 2013, 13 states and the District of Columbia had declared same-sex marriage legal,[1] and I began gestating the advantages of marriage: taking a stand, supporting the champions of marriage equality, garnering certain fiscal advantages, commanding recognition of our pairedness, and cementing our love. My thoughts were so unformed I didn't bring them up with John—nor he, if he had such thoughts, with me.

Finally, after cohabitation of nearly 40 years, on Valentine's Day, 2013, before a blazing fire and a bowl of crimson posies, I eased my arthritic knee onto a gardener's kneeling pad, looked John in the eye and asked, "Will you?" John could have said Not yet or Is that really necessary? But he said Yes.

We settled on a date and pondered a venue. Pennsylvania was statutorily dead set against same-sex marriage and didn't seem poised to change in the current millennium. Then, just in time, Delaware legislated marriage equality, and our sights turned to our Rehoboth Beach home and to our dock on the lake out front. Others had snapped their nuptial photos and paid for the privilege of being wed there. Why shouldn't we use the site ourselves?

(About the same time, the Supremes declared that Congress's Defense of Marriage Act, banning same-sex marriage, violated the equal protection clause of the Fifth Amendment; and they supported a federal judge's ruling that California's Prop 8, banning same-sex marriage, violated the U.S. constitution.[1])

We sent out a preliminary email invitation that read:

*.... Tom and John, to their own astonishment, have
decided the time has come to get married. Yes, to each
other. What with having happily tread water for almost
40 years, and with Delaware having just passed the
appropriate equality bill and the Supreme Court having
opened the way for accrual of federal benefits, it seems
right, even judicious.*

*So we're planning a party for the weekend of October 19,
with a short ceremony late Saturday afternoon on our
dock, followed by more party, dinner, more party, and
maybe even a breakfast party. And if you can come in
Friday, we'll get the partying started early.*

*Oh yes. The plan includes 9th District Court Judge
Vaughn Walker (ret.), the one who ruled California's
Prop 8 unconstitutional. He will officiate.*

This now-historic Vaughn Walker is the son of John's mother's
brother. That is, his first cousin.

For all the menu planning, food sampling, wine pairing, adjudi-
cating pick-up and drop-off spots for the wedding trolley, adjusting
wardrobes, attaching streamers to the dock, sending flowers to the
restaurant venues, assembling guest bags and trucking them around
to hotel rooms, picking up tuna canapés, baking cheese puffs, herd-
ing guests to the dock for the ceremony, re-herding them for pho-
tographs, and myriad other items that hinged on human compe-
tence—one or another of which could and in all probability should
have gone wrong—nothing does.

The centerpiece, of course, was that on an overcast, misty day,
water lapping under the dock on the lake, John and I wade into the
midst of 26 souls, all related by blood, marriage, or decades of wine.
They turn their beaming smiley faces toward us. Vaughn says some
words. We say some words back. Our respective brothers hand us
the rings, and we get them on each other's fingers without fum-
bling them into the lake. At the very end, we recite words of Dag

Hammarskjold which seemed custom-made for the extensive mileage already registered on our relationship's odometer ("For all that has been, thanks!") and for the exhilarant hope for more to come ("For all that will be, yes!").

Finally, we're this side of ritual and party, on a brief honeymoon in Provincetown, where it's cold, wet, empty, and somehow more charming than ever. Now is the time to ask ourselves if, as those certain friends had promised, we feel different after wedlock.

We aren't sure. Maybe it's too soon to tell.

As the weeks go by, people keep bringing the question back to us: "Does it feel different now?" We manage a mumbled "Guess so...."

I struggle to answer it for myself. Yes, I wear a wedding band. And I use the word husband publicly, in meeting people at cocktail parties, and with leverage, as when justifying why I should be sitting with John as he prepares for a brain shunt the next month. Is that different enough?

I feel the difference of relief—first, that we're overtly acknowledged as a love couple by our relatives and friends, and even by strangers with whom we happen to share our status. Second, relief that we're recognized as a joined couple under the law, and that whatever grace, blessing, or protection marriage affords hetero couples is afforded us.

I feel a little trepidation. The society that brought marriage equality into being cannot deny or escape the bonds of the institution, but neither can we.

I feel that I'm grown up and have at last been invited into a club that so many subscribe to–a club I scorned till I was asked to join. Now I can live the Cinderella fantasy like any other bloke—albeit a seriously remodeled fantasy.

I feel a political elevation, as if I—we—have taken the tiniest first step in publicly thanking the citizenry and the polity that enabled our twining, and the heroes of this astounding movement.

Do I feel more closeness, a greater sense of responsibility to the relationship? By this time, we've had 40 years to grow from a loosely coupled pair, when we kept our money separate and every little disagreement set me daydreaming of being single again, to a tightly coupled couple, with just about everything merged, where independence can't be defined except in adjectives of catastrophe and grief. I don't know that close can be closer than that, or more aching of responsibility.

But then, when I catch a glimpse of the wedding band on my hand or John's, I feel that a work forever on hold is now done, that the arc of us has at last grown into a complete circle.

[1]Wikipedia. "List of U.S. state constitutional amendments banning same-sex unions by type." Downloaded from the Web 2/7/2014.

[2]Levy, Ariel. "The Perfect Wife." *The New Yorker*, September 30, 2013, pp. 54-63

33

My Orphanage

Alone at last: losing my final parent.

Julian Barnes is as close to a contemporary literary hero as I've got. T. Coraghessan Boyle could be, just on the beauty of his name, but he's too unremittingly dark and cynical. Barnes mixes his light and dark writing and dishes up a large helping of irony. I've read most of his fiction and all of his non-fiction.

Last winter, a friend left behind Barnes' non-fiction *Nothing To Be Frightened Of*. In it, Barnes wields the arcane and thrillingly supple vocabulary of English like a mace as he contemplates his melancholy, even gruesome, obsession with death and dying. A list of his salient themes, from my reading, runs:

Barnes' fear of his own dying and dismissal of his own death,
The death and dying of others, especially the famous and literary,
The passive, pitiable life and untimely death of his father,
The life and tardy death of his insufferable mother,
Happy atheism, regular atheism, agnosticism, religion, and
*   irreligion,*
Philosophers morbid, morose, and moribund,
The art of writing and acceptance through writing,
Miscellaneous other weighty things.

By the middle of *Nothing* I realize that the book contains a multitude of nuggets, many so fine that they wash right through my large-bore (brain) pan, and that I have to buy my own copy, to re-read.

In the first quarter of the book, Barnes writes that when choosing authorship for a livelihood he decided to write as if his parents were dead. They were very alive at the time, but he needed to buffer himself from their provals, ap- or dis-, in order to get on with writing what he needed to write. The proof of that pudding being that, when he gave them a copy of his first novel, their reactions were late in coming and oblique (no eye contact; brief mention; dubious praise). Later in the book, however, Barnes admits that he always wrote as if he were trying to please his parents and that he does so even since his parents died, and that every writer does.

My first real writings—PhD thesis and subsequent professional publications—were not directed to Mom and Dad, but their approval was much in my mind, at least as I shared published copies. I didn't expect them to resonate with my first article, a sociological treatise on the future of public libraries; or my first book, a publication of my thesis on correlations of factors of library size and quality of services; or a scholarly article on the thesis; or a sociological survey replete with statistical mumbo-jumbo; or the rest of my professional oeuvre.

On the first journal article, Dad commented that he was pleased to see that I could write and went on to question certain punctuation. I don't think anything was ever said about my publications after that, except that they had gotten the latest one and Thank You.

Halfway through *Nothing* I also realize that I had never brought to consciousness the most important of my own dances with death and therefore wouldn't have a snowball's chance in hell of handling the topic of death, or even knowing if it needed handling.

So I look up orphanage, for that must be my topic: the death of my parents. Orphanage is defined inarguably as the place where an orphan is housed until he or she reaches some level of maturity. It is equally inarguably defined as the *state* of being an orphan, which is one of the things—perhaps the most important thing—I am. Moreover, if I nudge the word (good for Shakespeare, good for me) orphanage can embrace the *process* by which one becomes an orphan—which most simply means losing one parent, then the other or, most catastrophically, both at once. And it can include the change that occurs through grieving, resignation, recovery, and so on. Or even the lack of change, or fecklessness.

My mother died too early. She succumbed to a series of small heart attacks over several years and a final hopeless one, in May of 1983, at age 68 and a half, when I was almost 43. Too early not in that she was too young, although she was certainly that, but in that I was not ready.

It was too early for *me*. I had yet to shed the distancing and earned-independence posture that came on in my teens. I was still projecting an I'm-not-so-much-your-son-as-my-own-man attitude. Lord knows what I was protecting myself from: Mom and Dad were the least intrusive or demanding people I've ever known. In the vein of protectionism, the geographic gulf that had separated my parents and me once I reached adulthood—usually a couple thousand miles—felt comfortable to me, perhaps clarifying my need for emotional distance and freedom. We visited two to three times a year, in Florida or Philadelphia, and had a good time with each other. I engaged in standard rituals of love-of-mother—a brief hug and a kiss on greeting, a mother's day card, a birthday present, a phone call once every couple of weeks, and so on. These seemed real enough to me, and she seemed happy to accept them as valid demonstrations of son-love.

But I hadn't yet owned the fact that I truly loved her—hadn't opened myself to that, either in or out of her presence. Hadn't confessed that her contentment with how my life (and my brother's) had turned out was an endless source of contentment for me. Or how important her unbending love was—knowing it was there, forever, no matter what. But does anyone broach such feelings directly? "Hi Mom. Just called to thank you again for that unconditional mother-love." It would certainly have been a breach of family personality traits to expose feelings of such depth. As it was, if I had acted on my true feelings, I would probably have done nothing different, but the same things differently: visit her more, hang on the phone longer, draw out the details of her daily affairs, share more details of mine—just be with her more. At any rate, I didn't. I wasn't ready. And then she died, and my orphanage began.

Fifteen years later, when I was approaching 58, my orphanage (process) ended and my orphanage (state) was complete. Dad died about 14 months after his grandson, my nephew Tim (a general surgeon) fatefully observed, "Looking good, Grandpa! Losing some weight, I see." Which was prologue to getting him to a medic, pronto, who diagnosed multiple myeloma.

Losing my mother was numbing, from the moment Dad said over the phone, "Well, it's all over." I arranged for a substitute teacher for my Information and Referral course, cancelled committee meetings, and booked a flight to St. Petersburg. John stayed in Philadelphia to attend to his teaching and administrative duties and to our inn-keeping business.

I didn't quite know what I was feeling. Loss, yes; but on an abstract level. I was dry-eyed for the plane trip and the long cab ride from the airport. When Dad answered the door, we both exploded in wrenching sobs that went on for 20 or 25 minutes. I burst into tears whenever I approached someone whom I associated with Mom—my brother, my sister-in-law, Mom's neighbors—anyone. My brother, though obviously sad, was dry-eyed.

I flew home after the funeral and the tears stopped. But the hole in my gut came with me. It was a couple of years later that I noticed that I wasn't so empty and that I sometimes went days without thinking of her. And in a couple more years the emptiness was faint. I don't know when that happened—like a backache that you realize one afternoon hasn't been with you for a while.

By the time Dad's clock ran out, I thought Mom's death had

prepared me—acquainting me with grief in a depth I'd never experienced before, making me stronger in the face of loss, quelling the shock of irremediable absence. Maybe it had; maybe it hadn't.

Around 1994, Dad had moved to Gainesville, Florida, near my brother. One day Dick phoned to say that Dad's last blood transfusion didn't take hold like the ones before and that his kidneys were failing. I flew to Gainesville and cabbed to the hospital. When I walked into his room there was a small crowd—my brother Dick, Tim his son the surgeon, a couple of attendants. Dick said to Dad, "See, here's Tom!" Dad gave me a rheumy, vacant look and replied, "That makes it better." I took it that he knew he was dying.

Dick and I sat at his bedside for four days, spelling each other. Dad was weak, but responsive at first. As the days dragged on he became more laconic and his eyes remained closed. I tried to get him to talk—about his time in occupied Japan, about his early life on the farm, anything. He just grunted. I had to go back to Philadelphia on Thursday. The time came, I kissed him on the head, and said "I love you," the only time I declared that aloud. He didn't even grunt.

I flew to Philadelphia and the next day drove down to our place in Rehoboth. John and I were having dinner at home with two friends when the call came from my brother. "Dad died about half an hour ago," Dick said. He described a gentle exit. The last words from Dad, the ever-avid reader, were, "Dick, help me turn the page."

Dick was sad, but he wasn't crying. Me too. My heart was heavy, but my eyes were dry. I didn't feel the bottom drop out, as it had with Mom's demise—perhaps because, with Dad, I'd witnessed some of the dying process. At the memorial service, two months later, the small choir—coached by my brother and me on Dad's favorite hymns—launched into Rock of Ages. On the first chord, Dick and I broke down in tortured sobs.

Adult orphanage (the state) is arguable. True orphanage is considered a condition of youth. It's caricatured by Dickens' abused, impoverished, parentless street urchins, or even the invisible, institutionalized parentless child of today. The adult candidate for orphanage, on the other hand, may be worldly, well-to-do, a grand-mother, a board chairman. But loss and absence are there just the same. No matter how old the child, with the departure of that last and final parent go the only source of unconditional positive regard and the imagined but palpable shelter from the blind scythe of oblivion.

Fully orphaned I was with the death of Dad, and will be forever, standing here with my pal Julian Barnes, our toes curled over the edge of the bottomless black pit, being nudged ever so slowly forward by the ones next in line.

And I am writing this, as I must have written everything, for Mom and Dad.

That makes it better.

34

High

Finding ecstasy in dreams of flying.

I'm already twenty or thirty feet from the ground, before it strikes me that nothing is holding me up, that I'm flying on my own. I ascend slowly, straight up, into sky of gigantic grey and grey-blue brush strokes. My arms are at my side. I'm flossing my teeth. Yes, it is a dream.

Many writers, back to the ancients, have documented dreams of flying, chronicling frequencies, varieties, and impact on their lives.* I was surprised to learn this. Perhaps because dinner-table palaver with my friends and relatives has never gotten around to dreams, I don't know anyone who has dreamed of flying under their own power. They may have dreamed such dreams but failed to tell me. Or they may have had them but remembered nothing of them. I, too, in more than 25 thousand nights in the sack, could have dreamed thousands of flying dreams and remembered not a single one.

Happily to the contrary, I've had several that I do recall. Usually, I gain elevation deliberately, holding my arms out to the side and then bringing them straight down slowly, pushing against the air. Soft pressure builds between arm and torso and urges me into a slow, vertical take-off. My final altitude varies. Through that combination of will and hope that a dreamer uses in lucid dreaming, I urge the action along—Aah, way up! Or yes, yes, close to the ground today. And little beep beep beeps warning not too high or we'll wake up! I may elevate shrub high, tree high, or high to the point where a rowboat down below is the size of a cough lozenge. Once there, I may just hover and admire the sun-coated land, the glistening water, or the big sky straight ahead. Or I may set a direction, like a dark point in the sky or a cloudless sunny open spot, and move toward it—always slowly, perhaps for fear that I'll jolt the dream and wake up.

In an alternative flight pattern, I simply tilt forward, throw my feet out behind me as if going into a shallow dive, and follow the landscape horizontally. One time I buzzed the path of a creek, sliding in and out of the willows and cottonwoods—or maybe silver poplars—along the bank. I flitted from bank to bank, like a barn swallow chasing mosquitoes, swooping down close to the water, then backing off a few feet and hovering for a few seconds.

Another time, in a park of old oaks and pines, I elevated up into the canopies of several trees to remove dead limbs—large pine limbs with tan needles and oak limbs with shriveled brown leaves. That was the only purposeful flight I recall, probably triggered by an actual day out in the garden pruning large and small shrubs and trees. Usually I just revel in being airborne and gazing.

Flying under your own power requires concentration. In *The Hitchhiker's Guide to the Galaxy,* Douglas Adams prescribes, "There is an art to flying, or rather a knack. The knack lies in learning how to throw yourself at the ground and miss. ... Clearly, it is this second part, the missing, that presents the difficulties." So far, in my dreams, I've always missed, never fallen. I hold good gravity-free thoughts. I *believe.* If I don't, I remain earthbound, and my mind wanders off to some lackluster dream, like dancing radishes or lighting Lauren Bacall's cigarette or playing squash on a court filled with oak bureaus.

The possibility of free-fall injects only the merest quiver of anxiety into my flight. The real trajectory of my flying dreams is all serenity, detachment from earthly burdens, empowerment to act and achieve, optimism. When my flight comes to an end, lift evaporates and I settle back to earth. Or, as in the latest edition, the dream pixelates and vanishes. A couple of times my dream-flight happened near waking-up time. It virtually bounced me out of bed to a joyfully anticipated day and, a couple of beats later, the down-to-earth realization that there was nothing particular in that day to anticipate joyfully.

Years ago, when commercial aviation and I were both young, defying gravity via airplane delivered some of the miracle of self-propelled flying: a double serving of adventure and liberation, with a side of improbability. But thrill by plane has succumbed to the endless pile-on of bureaucratic hoops (like leg-room upgrades, carry-on limits, immutability of bookings, or trying to understand reward points); the cattle chutes of the boarding call; and the negative personal space once on board. The spirit of airplane flight has been and continues to be maximally compromised, and what is left behind is tribulation.

It is no wonder, then, why, like other flyboys and flygirls who carry the dream gene of self-powered aviation, I wait and wait till the gene clicks in once more and sets me free on my own wings.

*Havelock Ellis, "Aviation in Dreams," Atlantic Monthly, v. 106 pp 468-475, 1910. "Dreams of flying, and the dreams of falling with which they are sometimes associated, may fairly be said to be the best known and frequent type of dream."

35

Absolutely My Last Reflections on Mortality

Seeking comfort in the Barcalounger of decline and oblivion.

Pushed to enter, pulled to exit. The minute we're shoved out into life, oblivion is tugging from the other end, drawing us like fruit flies to that fatal saucer of sweet vermouth. We deny the undeniable with all our mental and emotional might for the whole journey; but at some point it becomes alarmingly clear where the moving sidewalk is carrying us.

For John and me, alarming clarity arrived the first week of December 2019.

The week started on a high. We had just committed to upgrading the functionality and, most importantly, the looks of the fifth and final bathroom in the Rehoboth Beach house. Renovation always raises our spirits. On the physical level, we love doing the design-and-buy, and we love watching cranial impulses materialize into a solid state. On the time-space level, a project grabs a piece of the future for us—almost as adamantly as taking out the original mortgage—and insists that we survive long enough to amortize the effort.

Wednesday. Demolition of the bathroom begins at 9 a.m. Later that morning we pick up the mail from our post office box and realize that demolition of a different kind had already begun.

There is a long hand-written letter from Ronnie Lowder, a once-was professional colleague who now lives in Palm Springs. It's a bad sign, for Lowder only resorts to manuscript form when things are complex and sensitive and the story is long. In this case, it was all of the above. His husband, George, who has a long history of seizures, impairment, and brain surgery, had tangled his feet in a kitchen chair and fallen. It landed him on the floor, hard, and then in the emergency room, intensive-care units, the operating room for new surgery on his head, and ultimately a nurse-assisted rehab center. This drama started over ten months ago, and George can just now walk to the bathroom, say some words, and eat mashed banana.

Thursday. Jared, the son of our backdoor neighbor in Rehoboth, Joanna, walks across the street to inform us that Joanna had been diagnosed with pancreatic cancer, likely metastasized to a lung: no treatment: final exit. Hospice oversight is in place. After years of bad health, she seems relieved to have a clear way out at 83.

Friday. John gets a call from Don, his family's handyman and yardman and friend-of-family for decades. He has a malignant testicular tumor.

Friday again. Jerry, a close professional friend in New York, informs us that he has prostate cancer. One additional death threat for a man who, by 74, has already endured a small stroke and heart surgery.

Sunday. Harry—real name Esme, but had gone by Harry for probably 80 of her 98 years, maybe because she was a force to be reckoned with in a man's world of big-business finance—was in Beebee Hospital with massive fluid retention complicating her various ills and threatening to do her in. She lives in the Moorings retirement complex outside Rehoboth Beach. I learn of her whereabouts when I present a poinsettia for her at the front desk of the Moorings and the desk attendant gives me the news.

I call Bonnie, another resident of the Moorings and a longtime friend of ours, to get the low-down. Bonnie, at 89, is the self-appointed care giver to her friend Harry/Esme. She tells me Harry's legs were grossly swollen and that she had insisted Harry check into the hospital.

And Bonnie has bad news of her own: her partner, Dee, 80, a chirpy, ageless beauty five years ago, is now in the memory care unit of the Moorings. She doesn't chirp much anymore. And the week after Dee was moved to memory care, their beloved bichon, Lacey, developed seizures and died. Now Bonnie doesn't even have the dog to go home to.

Come Sunday evening, the grout on the new bathroom floor is already dry enough to walk on. The disclosures of the week, bunching forcefully together, have us shaking our heads and swearing Damn-Hell-Shit-Fuck into the boiling pitch of our despair and the stinking realization that we are helpless. In the margins, we wonder at our own vanity-inanity-insanity in improving a nice enough and perfectly functional bathroom.

Similar close affairs of the flesh have been visited on us for a number of years now—although more tastefully spaced than the ones of this week—and have always seemed real. But they are getting realer and closer with repetition. Aside from the dalliances and diversions that we stuff into the fissures of our old age, they are what occupy us. We cannot block them out; we have no choice but to bond with their victims. We identify with Bonnie's loss of Dee's faculties and with Jerry's wary watch over his diseased prostate, and we ride the bad news to a closer relationship. We line up with our ailing friends, creaking arm in creaking arm, to high-kick our way—trundle our way, mostly—through the darkening realm of our latter days. We knit a new kind of comfort out of compassion and care, and proceed, together, under mostly cloudy conditions.

36

Chancing Upon
One's Inner Pineapple

Recognizing a force that's been driving us, all along.

You can go through life so occupied with living it—so focused on the screaming necessities of today, so overwhelmed with the social, political, and cultural storms gathering in the middle distance, and so obsessed with your financial security and family legacy at the horizon of your being—that you never look back to assess your life, to see how it moves from an old then to a new now, to discern a broad direction.

By "you," I mean "I." You and possibly everyone else in the world may regularly review their lives and assess their personal trajectories. The clerk at the CVS check-out counter may ask "How's your day been so far?" I have friends like that: "Been having a good week?" I don't know how to answer. They want me to take an on-the-spot pulse of my day or my week. These are probably the people who review their lives hourly for updates on where they're going and how successfully they're getting there.

OK for them, but that's not me.

A few months ago, midway through life's journey—really, more like three quarters of the way through—hell, four-fifths of the way—I was busy cranking out memoirish shorts. This required looking backward, of course, as I dredged up stuff about me and others to write about. And I did look backward, at the particulars of people and events and occasions and feelings and circumstances.

But in this fifteenth year of writing, up popped the question, "Where am I going with all this?" I looked back again, this time for a mega view of the adult me, as if tracking my past from a satellite. And there before my retrospecting eyes lay a defining thrust. It shouldn't have come as a surprise; it had been there all along. The undeniable theme, stamped in Times Roman script on a gleaming arc of my life, was hospitality.

So OK, by my own admission, much of the exertions and outcomes of my life could have been laid to things other than hospitality, like creature-comforting myself, or actualizing career ambitions, or investing wisely, or just plain keeping my hands out of the devil's pockets.

But if my life were a Wagnerian opera, an over-arching motif would be hospitality—making others welcome, comfortable, and worthy of special treatment. It motivates me and motivates us; John and I are in it equally, which may be why we have been together for a pretty long haul. Born in different months, we have nonetheless been operating for decades under the same sign of the zodiac: the Pineapple.

Starting around American colonial times, the pineapple became the symbol of hospitality. It was exotic by virtue of its otherworldly beauty and its rarity in the North American colonies and Europe. If it made the long sea voyage intact, a healthy specimen might become a loaner, moving from one household entertainment to another, a visual centerpiece of the festivity, symbolizing bounty, good cheer, and welcome until it rotted or got eaten by the owning family.

The pineapple spirit can be found in anyone: the Eagles fan treats the gal in the next seat to a Bud; the chairman of the book club raves about a new member's sweater; the seasoned hunter fist-bumps the novice hunter as he enters the duck blind for the first time. Everyone exercises hospitality some of the time.

My surprise in looking rearward is that John and I had let it—willed it—to consume the bulk of our time outside of our professional lives. It was our primary avocation. The hospitality genome was fully present and accounted for in our personal space, of course, when we entertained in the dining room or on the back deck. But it also extended to the five rental apartments inside our house at 42d street. Physically part of our house, furnished by us, and under our daily control, they qualified fully for our hospitality urges, as evidenced in physical environment—décor, quality of furnishings—and in a welcome carafe of wine in case they arrived after the state liquor store had closed and an "emergency start-up breakfast" of coffee, orange juice, homemade bread and jam.

It is largely hospitality that has led us to make things operable, convenient, dependable, comfortable, beautiful, harmonious, luxurious, kempt, delicious, well-orchestrated—the upshot being to create an enjoyable tarry for any fly that happens into our web.

It has called into play our endless enthusiasm and whatever talent we have for carpentry, electrical work, plumbing, painting, papering, repairing, construction; and justified our penchants for designing rooms, acquiring furnishings, setting a table, cooking well, and handing around good wine in good vessels: leaving that lucky guest—whether a dearest buddy or a barely known visitor—feeling a bit more like a royal after being touched by the pineapple.

About the Author

From a small town in southern Ohio, Tom Childers found his way to Washington DC and discovered his Midlantic soul. He picked up the degrees that turned him to the vocations of librarian and then career professor/dean of information studies. Outside of the office and classroom he plied the avocations of hospitality and inn-keeping. His primary stream of publications for about 30 years constituted social research on information service. This is his first work of creative non-fiction. Tom lives alternately in small-town Rehoboth Beach, Delaware and big-city Philadelphia with his husband of 47 years.

If you would like to contact Tom Childers you can do so at childers@drexel.edu.

Made in the USA
Middletown, DE
08 December 2020